between fathers & sons

Michael Smith, SJ

foreword by Joseph Telow, SJ

connorcourt
PUBLISHING

Fr Michael Smith, SJ, is a member of the Australian Province of the Society of Jesus. He is the Director of Campion Centre of Ignatian Spirituality in Melbourne, Australia, where he gives retreats to many different groups. He is also the Dean of Sentir Graduate College of Spiritual Formation, a college of the University of Divinity. Formerly the Rector of Jesuit Theological College in Melbourne, he has also taught in secondary school religious education programs.

Scriptural quotes are from the *New Revised Standard Version*.

Nihil Obstat: Reverend G. Diamond
    M.A. (Oxon), L.S.S., D. Theol.

Imprimatur: Reverend Monsignor G. A. Cudmore
    Vicar General

Given at East Melbourne, Vic., Australia on 23 November 1995

The *Nihil Obstat* and *Imprimatur* are official declarations that a book or pamphlet is free of doctrinal or moral error. No implication is contained therein that those who have granted the *Nihil Obstat* and *Imprimatur* agree with the contents, opinions, or statements expressed. They do not necessarily signify that the work is approved as a basic text for catechetical instruction.

© 2015 by Connor Court Publishing, Ballarat, Victoria.

All rights reserved. No part of this book may be used or reproduced in any manner whatsoever without written permission, except for materials appearing on pages labeled resource; and except in the case of reprints used in the context of reviews.

ISBN: 9781925138115

Photography: Nico Lariosa SJ

Printed and bound in Australia.

*To my father and mother,
Peter and Margaret,
thank you.*

Acknowledgments

I want to acknowledge the many people who have contributed in different ways to the writing of this manual.

I want to thank my late father, Peter, for being the kind and generous man that he was, and for showing me that compassion, warmth and unassuming service of others are manly qualities. I also want to thank him for instilling in me the virtue of perseverance, a virtue I needed to finish this project. And I want to thank my mother, Margaret, for her loving support and belief in me, and for imbuing me with the value of doing things properly, a trait that enabled me to return to the book and rewrite sections of it.

I am indebted to Fr Jim Colleran and the people of Our Lady of Lourdes Parish, Chicago, for the warm welcome and hospitality they extended to me while I was doing my research at Loyola University, Chicago.

I am deeply grateful to Dr Peter Gilmour and the late Dr Tad Guzie for their support and advice during my research. I want to especially mention the late Fr John Doyle SJ for the painstaking work he did in correcting, critiquing and editing the manual. His enthusiasm and encouragement were both needed and appreciated. I also thank Dr Anthony Cappello from Connor Court Publishing for his encouragement to republish this manual.

I am especially grateful to Fr Jim Colleran who co-facilitated the program with me in Chicago, Fr Leonard Moloney SJ who co-facilitated the program with me in Ireland, and Mr Simon Feely who has been my co-facilitator in Melbourne, Australia.

Finally, I wish to thank my Jesuit community at Xavier College in Melbourne for their support and encouragement.

Contents

Foreword vi

Introduction 1

Program Preparations 4

Foundations of the Program 9

Briefing Meeting for Fathers and Sons 19

Session One:
The Father and Son Bond 29

Session Two:
Becoming a Man 39

Session Three:
Dealing with Anger 51

Session Four:
Friendships with Girls and Women 61

Session Five:
The Quest for Identity 71

Session Six:
The Blessing Ritual 81

Appendix 91

Photocopy Resource Section 102

Foreword

Frontiers are sometimes physical borders and sometimes spiritual or even mystical boundaries. Adolescence is both. Every person has to live on both sides of it as it rolls through generation after generation. Perhaps the older and the younger in the golden past related across that rolling frontier amicably. Not today, and particularly not among males, as the shapes and forms of fathering have disintegrated one after another.

Commentators have given a name to this social illness: nonfeasance—the omission of an act which ought to have been performed. Fathers today are not sufficiently active in rearing their children, sons and daughters alike. And commentators have a partial cause of this illness staring up at them from their statistics: because marriage has somehow lost its bite, four of ten American children fall asleep at night in a house bereft of their biological father. Even where father lives with his family, pressures from gender role shifts, work patterns, urban mobility and anonymity, the drug culture, and a lot else have contrived to turn male adolescence into a fairly wild frontier.

Michael Smith, SJ, now Director of Campion Centre of Ignatian Spirituality in Melbourne, Australia, has boldly moved onto that frontier equipped with sound psychology and solid theology. He has created a series of group spiritual exercises that bring a father and his son together not at high noon—to put it this way—but in the cool of the evening where God walks. He has conducted the program in the United States and in Ireland as well as in his native Australia. It works.

In "Between Fathers and Sons" Fr. Smith outlines, as the book's subtitle puts it, "a program for sharing faith, strengthening bonds, and growing into manhood." The book lays out a program of six three-hour sessions, done on a weekend or spread out. Each session, grounded in an event from Jesus' life, incorporates brief input from the facilitator, individual reflection, group work, and time during which fathers and sons speak personally to each other.

Designed for adolescent males between thirteen and eighteen and their fathers (or someone who takes the father's place when he is not available to his son), the program is an excellent resource for pastoral teams in high schools, parishes, and retreat houses. "Between Fathers and Sons" offers much to pastoral counsellors and even to groups of fathers who wish to deepen their relationships with their sons.

The focus of "Between Fathers and Sons" raises some tangy questions about other relationships in the family: What about mother and daughter, for instance? Does that relationship need a program? For that matter, what about mother and son? While fathers and sons enhance their mutual relationship, do they leave mother out, or do they heighten all family relationships? Probably most of us would judge that in general, mother-son and mother-daughter relationships are in better shape than father-son or father-daughter relationships. Yet daughters need their fathers as much as sons need them. Perhaps therein lies Fr. Smith's next task: to apply the fine combination of gifts and skills he shows in this program to write a similar book for fathers and daughters.

Joseph Tetlow SJ

Introduction

The Mission

The *Between Fathers and Sons* program is designed for fathers and their adolescent sons. The mission of the program is to help and encourage fathers to foster the ongoing development of their sons into psychologically and spiritually-mature men.

The *Between Fathers and Sons* program is but a small step in the ongoing process of helping adolescent males grow into spiritually mature men whose lives are grounded in a personal relationship with Jesus Christ. As this is the aim, each session is rooted in the gospel; a time for prayer and personal reflection based on a gospel reading is integrated into each session.

The processes used during the program encourage open and honest dialogue between all the participants, especially fathers with their sons. The hope is that the father-son relationship will grow deeper, and each father will be encouraged to continue to nurture and nourish his son's growth into mature manhood after the program has concluded.

The program is *not* designed as therapy for a father and son whose relationship is severely disturbed. In such circumstances, a combination of family therapy and individual counselling with a professional therapist might be the best option.

Program Models

The *Between Fathers and Sons* program consists of a 90-minute briefing meeting and six three-hour sessions that can be delivered in a variety of ways:

- **A six-week program** One three-hour session per week is scheduled for six weeks. The manual is written with this format in mind, but the program is easily adapted to other formats.

- **A weekend retreat** The material for all six group sessions is covered during a period from Friday evening to Sunday afternoon. A timetable for a weekend retreat is included in the Appendix (see pages 92-93).

- **Three one-day workshops** This program is offered as three six-hour meetings, on three-consecutive Saturdays, for instance. Two group sessions are covered at each meeting. A timetable for the three-day program is offered in the Appendix (see pages 93-94).

Program Participants

This program can be conducted with any number of fathers and sons, provided there is enough support from other adults. The participants in the program and a definition of their roles are as follows:

Director of the program

This person is responsible for the overall organisation of the program. This includes promoting the program, contacting and registering the father and son participants, setting the dates for the sessions, finding an appropriate venue, and engaging and preparing suitable facilitators and small group moderators. The director co-ordinates the "Briefing Meeting for Fathers and Sons" (see page 19). The director may also serve as a facilitator for one or more sessions.

Facilitators

Two men working as a team facilitate the six sessions of the program. Experience has shown that the program works best with two facilitators who complement each other. It is taken for granted that the facilitators are men of faith who will reflect prayerfully on the mission of the program and seek to implement it in the best ways possible. Although some teaching experience and a basic understanding of developmental psychology would be helpful, the program allows for facilitation by men who are not professional teachers or counsellors. Facilitators may be drawn from, but are not limited to, the following sources:

- The religious education coordinator at a secondary school.
- Youth leaders or priests in a parish or neighbouring parishes.
- Counsellors in an outreach program for adolescent males.
- A group of fathers who wish to help their teenage sons through the period of transition into manhood.

Facilitators meet with the program director for orientation prior to the start of the program (see Preparation for Special Roles, page 5). Also, as a form of "apprenticeship" before serving as facilitators of the program, potential facilitators may be encouraged to serve at one or more sessions as small group moderators.

Small group moderators

These are men who do not have sons participating in the program. Their role is to guide the small group sharing which is integral to the program. Small group moderators are only necessary when there are more than eight fathers and eight sons in the program. (With a total of 16 or fewer father and son participants, the two facilitators also take the role of small group moderators.) The optimum size for each small group is eight: four fathers and four sons.

Fathers

Fathers usually attend the program with their sons. Nowadays, for a variety of reasons, many adolescent males do not live with their biological fathers. If at all possible, it is recommended that sons attend the program with their biological fathers. The program may effect some reconciliation between fathers and sons who are estranged.

Sons

Sons usually make the program with their fathers. The sons should be in the 13 to 19-year-old age range. The psychological and spiritual issues the program addresses are as relevant to 19-year-olds as they are to 13-year-olds. It is best, however, not to mix age groups. It is preferable that the adolescent participants be about the same age and from the same parish group, school year or even classroom.

Mentors

Those adolescents who cannot make the program with their fathers may attend with a mentor. A mentor is a man who substitutes for an adolescent's father, serving as a companion, confidant and model in the program and perhaps beyond. Mentors can be the father of another adolescent in the program, a stepfather, an uncle, a grandfather, an older adult brother, a family friend or a parishioner.

Grandfathers

A father and son may, if they want, invite a grandfather to participate in the program with them. He can be either the son's maternal or paternal grandfather. The inclusion of a grandfather adds an important generational dimension to the program. Often there is a very deep bond between grandfather and grandson that can be celebrated in the program. Sometimes the program can be a source of healing between a father and grandfather. At the *Briefing Meeting for Fathers and Sons* (see page 19) facilitators can mention this possibility.

Other Uses for the Manual

While this program is intended for use with fathers and sons meeting together, the material in *Between Fathers and Sons* can be adapted for use in other settings. Sessions One through Five can be easily used with adolescents in a variety of religious education settings. For example, a teacher wanting to explore with teenage students the issues of anger and aggression will find enough material from Session Three to lead four 45-minute class periods.

The material in the manual can be used as the basis for a youth retreat, or adapted for use at a retreat for men, the majority of whom are fathers.

Program Preparations

To prepare to use the *Between Fathers and Sons* program, the following steps and procedures are recommended.

Promoting the Program

The concept of fathers and sons meeting together in an extended program of this kind is relatively new. One of the most challenging tasks for the coordinator is to explain the program to a wide audience of adolescents, fathers, mothers and the parish or school community. Initial resistance to the program often focuses in the following areas: *a wounded bond between father and son* and *peer group pressure among adolescents*. In the author's experience, these concerns disappear once the fathers and sons begin the program. A coordinator can address these issues and encourage participation in several ways:

- If there is a rift between a father and son, there is likely to be a reluctance to attend this program on the part of both. Participating in the program does pre-suppose that fathers and sons will open themselves emotionally. Even fathers and sons with a healthy relationship initially tend to find this aspect threatening. Paradoxically, the possibility that the program might prompt and assist fathers and sons to address interpersonal issues that they might not otherwise be inclined to face is a very attractive proposition for both. Experience shows that fathers particularly want to enhance their relationships with their sons. The structured format provides a means to do so.

- Adolescents are strongly connected to their peer group. Trying anything new or counter to the group is usually taboo for adolescents. A way to offset this issue is to directly target adolescent peer group leaders and their fathers for participation. This will make it easier for other adolescents to join the program. If individual adolescents are reluctant to attend, invite them to register with a friend so that they are assured of knowing at least one person in the program.

- Mothers are often the ones who first see the need for the program and who prompt their husbands and sons to attend. Addressing mothers through parish groups, religious education programs and school communications is a helpful starting point.

- Fathers and sons who have attended the program are generally pleased with the experience and its results. These former participants can be solicited to offer testimonials about the program before groups of their peers.

- Announce the program to the parish or school community. The parish bulletin is one means, but also ask the parish priest to explain the program and encourage sign-ups as part of the announcements at Mass. Set up a table outside the church to register participants and offer a timetable for the briefing meeting and sessions.

- Personal invitation remains the most effective of promotional means. Assemble a team of helpers to call fathers and invite them to attend the program with their sons. Visit classrooms, youth groups and sports training to likewise personally invite adolescents.

Note: Unnumbered pages 98-99 in the Photocopy Resource Section is a format for a flyer with a synopsis of each session and a place for you to record the dates, times, and meeting place of the program. Photocopy the two pages back-to-back and fold accordingly.

Preparation for Special Roles

There are several special roles in the program that require preparation prior to participation. The director of the program is responsible for communicating important preparation tasks to the appropriate participants listed below.

Facilitator Preparation

Two men working together facilitate each session. It is strongly recommended that each facilitator has his own copy of this manual and reads and becomes thoroughly familiar with the foundational principles of the program and the content and process of each of the sessions. Background information for each session is specifically designed to help orient facilitators. Also, in order to be more effective, it is suggested that facilitators pay special attention to these attitudes and skills:

- **Personal reflection** To prepare, each facilitator needs to reflect on the issues that will be covered in the program, and how they apply to his own life. For example:

  — his own transition to manhood;

  — his relationship with his father;

  — if he is a father himself, his relationship with his son;

  — key experiences in his own spiritual journey;

  — how he deals with anger and any tendencies he has toward violence;

  — his attitudes toward sexuality;

  — his relationships with women;

  — his goals and aspirations;

  — his image of God and his relationship with God.

  The method that each facilitator uses to reflect on these issues will vary. He may choose to discuss these issues with the other facilitator or a close friend; he may pray; he may write a journal; or he may talk with a priest or counsellor. Whatever methods he chooses, it is important that each man face these issues. His personal reflection will help him identify with and understand the growth issues the fathers and sons will be asked to face, and deepen his capacity to respond to them with empathy.

- **Interpersonal skills** The program facilitators should be well-practiced in basic listening and communication skills. But, more than this, they need to respond with empathy and care to the fathers and sons in the group.

- **Effective working relationship with one another** The facilitators need to be aware of each other's strengths and weaknesses. For example, one person may be more comfortable leading prayer, another in disseminating content material. The sessions are more effective when facilitators work from their individual strengths.

- **Prayer** Prayer is vital to the program's success. Facilitators should spend time individually reading and reflecting on each session's material in the days before the scheduled date, calling on the Holy Spirit for inspiration. It is also beneficial if they share their individual reflections with one another or, if that is not possible, with a spouse or a trusted friend.

- **Collaboration with the participants** A good rapport is needed not only between the facilitators themselves, but also between the facilitators and father and son participants. This attitude is expressed in the phrase "we are on this journey together", rather than "we have all the answers". Collaboration entails listening carefully and respecting the ideas of all—adults and adolescents—and incorporating them into the program when possible.

- **Working knowledge of the program** The facilitators are expected to have a basic understanding of the hypotheses and anecdotal evidence on which this program is based. The "Foundations of the Program" section (pages 9-17) offers a synopsis, focusing on these areas:

    — a basic understanding of the process of transition to manhood for males in an industrialised urban society;

    — an appreciation of the psychosocial and religious development of adolescent males and middle-age males;

    — some background knowledge of developmental psychology.

- **Presentation skills** Each session includes short presentations to be given by the facilitators. The facilitators should not read these scripts or attempt to commit them to memory. Rather, they should brief themselves on the presentations and express them in their own words and style. Facilitators are also strongly encouraged to include short personal stories where possible to illustrate the subject matter.

Small Group Moderator Preparation

Much of the sharing in the *Between Fathers and Sons* program is done in small groups with an equal mix of fathers and sons. These groups should be pre-assigned by the coordinator and facilitators and remain the same throughout the program. Continuity in membership helps build a sense of sharing and trust.

The association of adults and adolescents in any situation is likely to be awkward and have its difficult moments. In this setting, where the expectation is that the participants will be open to share the most important memories, dreams, and values of their lives, it is vital for the moderator to work toward establishing a comfortable and trusting atmosphere. Resource 6, "Guidelines for Small Group Sharing", offers guidelines to be presented to adolescents and fathers. Listed below are some other basic suggestions for small group moderators:

— Ask the group to pledge confidentiality of what is shared. The rule is: "What is said here, stays here."

— Be sure to allow for a pre-response before small group sharing. A full five minutes is recommended for the participants to consider the questions provided in this program.

— Designate the first speaker; for example, "Mr. Brown, let's begin with you." Then move around the group giving everyone a chance to share.

— Always allow a "pass" option. The participants must know that anytime they don't know how to answer or don't want to answer publicly, they don't have to. Move the dialogue gradually from light, easy topics to more serious ones.

— Emphasise the importance of *listening*. For adolescents, especially, the dynamic of the group may initially be an intimidating one. They need to know that neither the moderator nor their fathers will use the occasion to moralize or pass judgment on their comments. Rather, these sessions are intended to explore all sides of an issue.

— The moderator's job is to move the sharing along. Resist the urge to offer closing statements to each person's response.

Speaker Preparation

A well-received part of the program is the short five to 10 minute prepared talks given by pre-selected fathers and sons at specific sessions. These talks are designed to personalise the subject matter so that it can be more easily understood by both adolescents and adults and to encourage a similar sharing by all in the small groups.

Guidelines for preparing each talk are included in the Appendix. It is recommended that you target potential father and son speakers for specific talks early in the program. In the session prior to the session when the talk is to be given, provide copies of the appropriate resource to each chosen speaker. The following chart allows you to plan for these talks for the entire program:

Topic	Given By	When	Resource
The Father-Son Bond	two fathers	Session 1	4
Dealing with Anger	two fathers and their sons	Session 3	12
Friendships with Girls and Women	two fathers	Session 4	16
The Quest for Identity	three sons	Session 5	19

Pre-Session Casual Meals

If the program is run in the evening, for instance starting at 7 pm, it is very helpful to begin with a casual meal for the fathers and sons at 6 pm. This arrangement allows the participants to mix socially for an hour beforehand, and helps build a sense of community. It also helps punctuality, that is, it gives those fathers who must travel some distance sufficient travelling time to ensure that they arrive sometime before 7 pm. Beginning with a meal means that the session is more likely to start on schedule and with everyone present.

The meals are "casual", meaning that the participants themselves take responsibility for bringing salads, main courses and desserts. If possible, arrange for the parish or school to provide utensils and drinks. Resource 3, "Casual Meal Sign Up", will help coordinate what will be brought for each meal. It is recommended that one small group per session be assigned clean-up duty.

Please do not underestimate the benefits of trust and camaraderie that develop during this mealtime. This type of spirit is essential to the program. However, if you feel the regular casual meal is impossible for your program, adapt as necessary. For example, you may have a casual meal at the first and last sessions or shorten the social time to a half hour of snack foods prior to the beginning of the session.

Settings

The *Between Fathers and Sons* sessions use a variety of settings. In an ideal situation, all of the following kinds of spaces would be used. Of course, you will have to adapt to the space you have available.

Dining area This is essential if the session is going to begin with a casual meal. It is recommended that each table have enough seats for all the members of one small group. A cafeteria-style buffet table is also recommended.

Large-group presentation area A room large enough to hold all the participants comfortably is needed. Chairs are needed for all participants. A white board or a blackboard are also required in this room.

One-to-one spots Each session includes time for one-to-one sharing between father and son. Ideally this could occur in the large-group presentation area, as long as there can be at least six feet between each father and son pair, so that their sharing is private.

Small-group discussion spaces Because the large group of fathers and sons will be split into a number of smaller groups during each session, it will also be helpful to have a fewer smaller rooms with comfortable chairs in which small-group sharing can occur.

Liturgical area This will only be needed during Session Six, "The Blessing Ritual". If a chapel is available, it may be suitable for the ritual. It may also be appropriate to have the ritual in the large-group presentation area or in the sanctuary of the church.

Supplies

A specific supply list is included for each session. The following are items needed for every session:

- a white board or blackboard;
- erasable marker pen or chalk;
- pens or pencils for each participant;
- a photocopier.

Advance Preparation

Long-term planning is necessary for the individual meetings and sessions. The contents of this entire manual should be previewed by the program coordinator. All session plans should be previewed by the facilitators. Supplies should be compiled, settings arranged, and special preparations made prior to the start of the course.

Foundations of the Program

The *Between Fathers and Sons* program is based on four foundational principles:

- The importance of a father's involvement with his son, especially during adolescence.
- The need for male initiation rituals.
- A father's role in nurturing his son's faith.
- The father-son relationship in Erikson's life development schema.

1. The Importance of a Father's Involvement with His Son, Especially During Adolescence

A father's active presence is crucial for his son's development, especially in adolescence. Today, however, the father-son bond is one of society's most damaged and damaging relationships. Many fathers are physically or psychologically absent from their families, often with tragic results.

Despite the influence of the women's movement, parenting in most modern families remains organised asymmetrically so that the mother is the primary caregiver and the father is more remote, often due to his pursuit of career success and financial stability. This program is based on the principle that it is absolutely necessary for fathers to assist in the developmental growth of their adolescent sons in order to help them to become mature men. Without a father's assistance, the son is more likely to grow up with a limited sense of what it means to be a man. Also, the failure of fathers to initiate their sons into manhood is a source of deep and lasting woundedness in the father-son relationship.

Historical factors that influence the father-son relationship

Has the father-son bond always been wounded, or is this a relatively new phenomenon in human history? While it is hard to establish exactly what the father-son relationship was like in earlier ages, there is evidence that structural changes in the way industrialised societies have organised their economies have had a major impact.

Robert Bly, who explores the father-son relationship in his book *Iron John*, suggests that the Industrial Revolution was a significant turning point in the relationships between fathers and sons. Bly points out that before the Industrial Revolution, a son participated in what his father did. He worked with his father. He shared in his father's world. He saw what his father did and how he spent his time. Bly contends that because they worked together, the son felt validated by his father. That is, a son did not have to spend the rest of his life *earning* his father's respect, because he already had it. He already had a domain in which he had credibility, in which he was accepted, in which he knew he had gifts. In short, he didn't have to prove himself as a man.

This sort of family economy where a father trained his son, and then worked with him, existed in rural Europe and America until the end of the 18th century when the Industrial Revolution wrought huge changes in societal and family structures. Father and son business partnerships disappeared as men, women, and children began working in factories and mines. The hours and the conditions under which they worked disrupted the then-existing patterns of family life.

As the work situations have continued to evolve, sons now have less access to their fathers than they did 200 years ago. Fathers are often precluded from child-rearing by a work routine that takes them out of their homes for much of the day and into the night. As a result, a void has developed in the father-son relationship because sons don't see how their fathers behave, react and cope at their workplace, so they don't really know who their fathers are. This lack of sufficient and meaningful contact with their fathers is detrimental to the sons' development of a healthy masculine self-image. Consequently, when these adolescents grow to manhood, many of them have a false or insufficient understanding of what it means to be a man. They define themselves by career, status, and possessions—in other words, by what they do, who they know, and what they own, rather than by who they are. This, in turn, affects their relationships with their wives, with their daughters, with other men and women, and, particularly, with their own sons.

This program encourages a conversation between fathers and sons that will in great part repair this lack of communication between fathers and sons.

2. The Need for Male Initiation Rituals

An examination of male initiation rituals in tribal societies reveals their effectiveness in leading adolescent males to a mature sense of gender identity according to tribal custom and practice. Tribal initiation rituals generally involve these elements:

- removing the pubescent youth from familiar surroundings;
- differentiating him appropriately from the world of his mother;
- proving him worthy of manhood through the test of challenges and ordeals;
- allowing him to experience the spirit world;
- accepting him into the community of men;
- returning him to the tribe as a man.

Recent literature on male psychology and spirituality suggests that adolescent males in industrialised urban societies also need some form of ritual initiation. Like their counterparts in tribal cultures, they need a way to mark the end of boyhood and the beginning of manhood. Initiation rituals help meet the psychological, spiritual and developmental needs of young males as they make this transition. Male initiation rites also meet the adolescent male's need for belonging, acceptance, and validation by older males. In industrialised urban societies, unfortunately, initiation is usually left to chance, and in most cases adolescent males search for a way of fulfilling these needs and proving their manhood by themselves—an almost impossible and often dangerous task.

Society's need for male rites of passage

There is a great need today for fathers to initiate their adolescent sons into a spiritually mature and responsible manhood. Richard Rohr and Joseph Martos, in their book, *The Wild Man's Journey*, identify various societal ills that they connect, in part, to the lack of male initiation rites available today:

> The pattern [of initiation] was so widely documented that one is amazed that we have let go of it so easily. The contemporary experience of gangs, gender identity confusion, romanticisation of war, aimless violence and homophobia will all grow unchecked, I predict, until boys are again mentored and formally taught by wise elders. Historically, it was much of the meaning of the medicine man, the priest and the shaman. Now boys look to coaches, drill sergeants and fundamentalist preachers for what the Church no longer gives them.[1]

Much of the aimless violence Rohr and Martos cite is perpetrated by adolescent males, and the incidence of violence among adolescent males is increasing. For example:

- Each year in Australia, one out of every 20 juveniles is arrested for a property or violent crime.[2]
- Juvenile (that is, children between the ages of 10 and 16) arrest rates in Victoria for violent crimes has increased by more than 250 per cent over the past 20 years.[3]
- Arrest rates for males is four times that of females in Australia.[4]

Early adolescence is the stage at which males attempt to prove themselves as men. That some strive to achieve a sense of manhood in antisocial and violent ways is not surprising. One factor, among a constellation of social factors, contributing to this upsurge of violence is that younger males are not being taught by older males about how to deal with their aggression and curb their violent tendencies. Rather, many adolescents seek membership in non-productive groups like gangs that ironically tap into an adolescent's need for initiation, yet do not typically answer his spiritual hunger. These types of pseudo-initiations may also be found as part of socially acceptable organisations like the armed forces.

Also, the increase in abuse and exploitation of women by young males is another indicator that there is a troubled group of young men in society who have not learned how to be sexually mature and responsible men. Initiation rites help to this end.

The Eternal Boy

There is an increasing appearance in modern society of the eternal boy—the adult male who has not fully reached his manhood, but is trapped in boyhood. In *King, Warrior, Magician, Lover*, Robert Moore and Douglas Gillette use the term "Boy psychology" to describe the eternal boy. They write:

> What happens to a society if the ritual processes by which these (gender) identities are formed become discredited? In the case of men, there are many who have had no initiation into manhood or who had pseudo-initiations which failed to evoke the needed transition into adulthood. We get the dominance of Boy psychology. Boy psychology is everywhere

around us, and its marks are easy to see. Among them are abusive and violent acting-out behaviours against others, both men and women; passivity and weakness, the inability to act effectively and creatively in one's own life and to engender life and creativity in others (both men and women); and, often, an oscillation between the two—abuse/weakness, abuse/weakness.[5]

This widespread expression of the eternal boy by immature men who have not been appropriately guided into manhood threatens the social fabric of society.

A spiritual context for initiation

The *Between Fathers and Sons* program offers an initiation process for adolescent males situated firmly in a spiritual context. Why? Spiritual transformation is at the heart of an adolescent male's transition into manhood. In indigenous cultures, initiation into manhood is seen primarily as spiritual transformation. Mircea Eliade, the world-renowned expert on myth and symbolism, writes:

> Initiation represents one of the most significant spiritual phenomena in the history of humanity. It is an act that involves not only the religious life of the individual, in the modern meaning of the word "religion"; it involves his *entire* life. It is through initiation that, in primitive and archaic societies, man becomes what he is and what he should be—a being open to the life of the spirit, hence open to the culture into which he was born. For as we shall soon see, the puberty initiation represents above all the revelation of the sacred—and, for the primitive world, the sacred means not only everything that we now understand by religion, but the whole body of the tribe's mythological and cultural traditions.[6]

For thousands of years, adolescent males in indigenous cultures have been initiated into the spirit world by their fathers and the older men of their group. During their initiation, the sacred stories and cultural traditions of the tribe that pertain to men, and which were formerly hidden from the boys, are finally revealed to them. Hearing the stories is a sign that they are now regarded by the community as men.

Likewise, contemporary adolescent males need a revelation of the sacred as they make their passage into manhood in a modern industrial culture. The modern adolescent needs his father to guide him to spiritual awareness. Hence participation in this program allows fathers the opportunity to share their spiritual experiences, and to help the adolescent males in the group to grow into spiritually mature men whose lives are grounded in a personal relationship with Jesus Christ, and whose actions are guided by the ethical principles found in the gospel.

Because authentic masculine rites of passage in western culture are virtually non-existent, and because the bonds between adolescent males and their fathers tend, in general, to be strained or absent, the task for fathers of addressing an adolescent's need to grow into psychologically and spiritually mature manhood is formidable. This program goes some way toward addressing this need.

3. A Father's Role in Nurturing His Son's Faith

A man recalled that as a small boy he passed his father's bedroom door one morning and saw his father, still in his pyjamas, kneeling beside his bed, praying. This image had a tremendous effect on him. For the first time in his life he realised that prayer was something men could participate in, whereas previously he had seen prayer as a feminine domain—that is, something only his mother did. His father was a private man, but catching him praying showed the son that his father had a relationship with God. And, as a male like him, he too could relate to God in prayer.

This is a familiar story. While there is little hard, empirical evidence to support the hypothesis that fathers play a crucial role in transmitting faith to their sons, similar recollections of many men imply that the example of a father's spirituality is crucial to his son's belief in God. The *Between Fathers and Sons* program is based on the anecdotal evidence of a number of men that their fathers played a crucial role in transmitting faith to them, and in nurturing their spiritual development.

Faith is about relationships; specifically, the relationships of people with God and of people with other people. It is in relationships that faith is shared—through observing the attitudes, outlooks and actions of significant people toward one another, and, by inference, toward God. For example, the son observes the relationship of his father toward others (the horizontal dimension of faith) and makes assumptions about his father's relationship to God (the vertical dimension of faith).

This program allows for adolescents to meet with, listen to and talk to their fathers and other fathers from the Christian community who have sought, in various ways, to embody lives of faith and service. When fathers share with sons their struggles, and their experiences of God in the midst of those struggles, they in effect show their sons how to find meaning for their lives. They communicate the attitudes and orientations that have helped them to make sense of their lives and have given them direction. This is a vital task for any father who has a son approaching manhood.

4. The Father-Son Relationship in Erikson's Life Development Schema

Psychoanalyst Erik Erikson proposed a schema for human psychological and social development that states that development occurs throughout life. At each stage, people strive to adapt to changes in themselves, in their environment, and in their relationships in order to attain a healthy sense of self.

Erikson nominated eight predetermined stages of development. Psychosocial development begins with the initial relationship of the infant with his or her mother, which, if the relationship is good enough, engenders in the infant a sense of basic trust. If infants' needs are not met or are rejected, they learn to be fearful of the world and develop a sense of mistrust. The other stages are affected by the results of this conflict between trust and mistrust. New conflicts arise at each stage. According to Erikson, failure at one stage may hinder the achievement of a healthy sense of self at later stages. Erikson's eight stages of life development are listed on page 14.

MATURE ADULTHOOD								INTEGRITY VERSUS DESPAIR
MIDDLE ADULTHOOD							GENERATIVITY VERSUS STAGNATION	
YOUNG ADULTHOOD						INTIMACY VERSUS ISOLATION		
ADOLESCENCE (12 to 18)					IDENTITY VERSUS IDENTITY CONFUSION			
SCHOOL AGE (6 to 11)				INDUSTRY VERSUS INFERIORITY				
PLAY AGE (3 to 5)			INITIATIVE VERSUS GUILT					
EARLY CHILDHOOD (1 to 3)		AUTONOMY VERSUS SHAME AND DOUBT						
INFANCY (0 to 1)	BASIC TRUST VERSUS BASIC MISTRUST							
					SONS		FATHERS	

14   *Between Fathers and Sons*

Normal psychosocial development has a definite direction through these eight stages, each of which builds on the prior stage. For Erikson, growth comes through resolving relational conflicts with one's parents and others. Successful negotiation of a conflict leads the person onto the next stage of psychosocial development.

A co-development model

Erikson's life development schema is important for this program because fathers and sons are at different life stages. For this reason, the design of the *Between Fathers and Sons* program utilises a co-development model. The program simultaneously addresses the different psychosocial and spiritual tasks of adolescent sons and middle-aged fathers, paying attention to:

- the task of the adolescent stage, *the achievement of a coherent sense of personal identity*. Adolescents are concerned with the question of who they are, and who they will be as adults;

- the task of the middle-age stage, *generativity*. Generativity is another name for the care, nurturance, and guidance of the next generation.

The sections below explore more information about these developmental tasks as related to the adolescent sons and middle-aged fathers enrolled in this program.

Achieving identity

The psychosocial task facing an adolescent male is the achievement of a coherent sense of personal identity. Identity achievement involves a synthesis of his past self-definitions, his present experiences and his future aspirations. The *Between Fathers and Sons* program is designed to help each adolescent male reflect deeply on his life story and dare to say where his life story might lead him.

Achieving personal identity is a relational process. The powerful influence of a peer group notwithstanding, an adolescent's relationship to his parents is the most important contributor to his identity. An adolescent with a poor relationship with his parents will tend to require constant reassurance from them, and have difficulty in gaining a clear sense of who he is. Many adolescent males report that they can talk freely with their mothers but find communication with their fathers awkward or difficult. Hence the emphasis in this program on improving the relationship a son has with his father.

Identity and spirituality

From a Christian perspective, achieving a coherent personal identity also involves a relationship with God. A person's relationship with God is associated with *vocation*. Vocation comes from a Latin word that means "call". In this sense, achieving a coherent personal identity involves hearing and answering God's call. The call of God initiates the adolescent male into his identity and provides him with a sense of his ultimate purpose.

The task, then, for an adolescent male, is to discern God's call in his life. This is not an easy thing to do. Clarity in understanding God's purposes is rare. The adolescent male will find himself drawn in many different directions, not all of which are life-giving. He may, for instance, be seduced by materialism, enticed into the drug culture, beguiled by alcohol, tempted to exploit young women and so on. The guidance he receives from his father can help him negotiate his direction lest he make poor choices in life.

A habit of prayer and reflection is also beneficial. Through prayer, the adolescent gradually becomes attuned to the presence of God in his life, and, little by little, he will develop a sense of God's will in his life, which is synonymous with his truest identity. God's will ought not be viewed as something imposed from the "outside"—some divine blueprint that an adolescent has to follow. Rather, God asks him ". . . to act justly, to love tenderly and to walk humbly with God" (Micah 6:8). God wants him to be fully alive; as Saint Irenaeus expressed it, "The glory of God is a person who is fully alive."

Religious development of an adolescent

Another factor affecting an adolescent's personal identity is his religious development. A shift in religious thinking usually occurs during adolescence, paralleling the identity crisis typical of this period. For adolescent males, this stage of religious development is characterised by questioning, doubt and religious searching. Uncertainty is usually the distinguishing characteristic of an adolescent male at this stage of his religious development. He needs support as he critically examines the religious beliefs that sustained him through boyhood. The *Between Fathers and Sons* program is designed to gently prompt each adolescent to reflect on his previously-held religious beliefs, and to assist his transition from the religious thinking of boyhood toward the self-chosen faith of manhood, which involves asking mature questions and making mature choices.

Fatherhood and generativity

According to Erikson, the psychosocial crisis that unfolds in middle adulthood involves generativity versus stagnation (see table, page 14). The *Between Fathers and Sons* program is specifically designed to assist fathers in their generative task. Fathers are asked to care for the next generation by fostering the ongoing development of their sons and the other adolescent males in the group into psychologically and spiritually mature manhood. The program asks of a father a continuing emotional investment in and nurturing of his adolescent son as he grows into manhood.

Ideally, fatherhood is always generative. However, in many cases fathers exhibit the negative pole of this developmental stage—*stagnation*. Many fathers find themselves unable to invest emotionally in their sons. Some fathers, because their lives have been impoverished through their own lack of fathering, tend toward a self-preoccupation that precludes ongoing interest in their sons. A father's abdication of his generative role in the identity struggles of his son may perpetuate a generational problem. The likelihood is that his son will also abrogate *his* responsibility to *his* son in middle adulthood.

Because many fathers today are not guiding their sons, some mothers, particularly those in single parent families, find they are burdened with the responsibility themselves. This is not a responsibility a mother is naturally equipped for, or ought be expected to handle alone. One of the developmental tasks of a son during adolescence is to differentiate himself appropriately from the feminine identity of his mother. A father can support his son through this period. But if the responsibility for guiding a boy through his transition into manhood rests chiefly on his mother, the differentiation process becomes problematic. To whom does he look for emotional support as he is reframing his relationship with his mother? Where does he look for role models?

If, however, a father takes an active role in initiating and guiding his son into manhood, not only will he be facilitating his son's achievement of gender identity, but he will also be moving toward achieving the task of his own developmental stage, which is the generative guiding of the next generation.

One of the best ways in which a father can be truly generative is by providing his son with a glimpse of his own ethical framework and spiritual experiences. A father cannot coerce his son to adhere to his own religious and ethical values. A son must encounter the mystery of God firsthand and fashion his own moral codes that flow from his own encounter with God. But if a son perceives his father's faith to be authentic and alive, the shared experience is indeed generative.

Briefing Meeting Fathers

Background Information for Coordinator and Facilitators

The "Briefing Meeting for Fathers and Sons" orients the participants to the process and content of the program. It also allows fathers and sons to briefly examine their relationship with one another, with the understanding that the issues introduced at this meeting will be covered in more depth in the succeeding sessions. This meeting should be held after the program has been promoted and registrations have been taken. However, this meeting should be an opportunity for both fathers and sons to reflect more intently on whether or not this program is right for them. Also, in observing those who attend this meeting, you may notice some who are especially reticent about participating. Or, you may discover adolescents who are disruptive and uncooperative to such an extent that they disrupt the group. Use the time after the meeting to speak with any father and son pairs who have doubts about their own participation and interview them about these concerns. Speak also to any fathers and sons whose behaviour concerns you. It is not wise to allow any unwilling or poorly behaved participants to inhibit the success of the whole group.

The coordinator of the program and two facilitators all have roles in this meeting. The coordinator leads the "Gathering and Greetings", "Gospel Reflection" and "Announcements". The facilitators share the lead in the other parts of the meeting. During a writing and sharing period, the fathers and sons meet separately with one facilitator leading each group. The entire meeting is about 90 minutes long. It should take place approximately one week before Session One.

Pastoral Response

The purpose of this session is to:

- welcome the fathers and sons and orient them to the content and process of the program.

Supply List

For this meeting you will need:

- name tags;
- index cards;
- a supply of pens or pencils;
- copies of Resource 1, "Fathers and Sons Program Timetable" (with times and dates filled in);
- copies of Resource 2, "Father and Son Information Sheet" (one for each pair; cut on dashed line);
- one copy of Resource 3, "Casual Meal Sign Up";
- two copies of Resource 4, "The Father and Son Bond".

Meeting Outline

Gathering and Greetings (about 10 minutes)

Gospel Reading (about 10 minutes)

Small Group Surveys (about 20 minutes)

Survey Roundup (about 10 minutes)

Father and Son Sharing (about 10 minutes)

Overview of Program (about 15 minutes)

Program Announcements (about 10 minutes)

Conclusion (about 5 minutes)

Gathering and Greetings

(about 10 minutes)

Arrival/Welcome

Greet the fathers and sons as they arrive. Ask them to print their names on name tags and have a seat in the large meeting room. When everyone has arrived, introduce yourself and briefly explain your role in the program. Then, say:

Welcome to this briefing about the *Between Fathers and Sons* program. We have invited you here for a number of reasons:

- to introduce ourselves to you and to help you begin to get to know one another before the program begins;
- to tell you about the topics we will address and how we will address them in the six sessions of the program;
- to initiate dialogue between the adults, between the teens, and between the fathers and sons;
- to make some announcements important to the success of the program.

Introduction of Facilitators

Introduce the facilitators who will lead the six sessions of the program. Allow each facilitator a couple of minutes to address the group, stating briefly his hopes and expectations for the program.

Gospel Reading

(about 10 minutes)

Luke 1:11-18

Introduce and read the story of the angel who appeared to Zechariah. Say:

This is the story about a man called Zechariah—the father of John the Baptist—and the prophecy the angel makes to him about his unborn son:

Then there appeared to him an angel of the Lord, standing at the right side of the altar of incense. When Zechariah saw him, he was terrified; and fear overwhelmed him. But the angel said to him, "Do not be afraid, Zechariah, for your prayer has been heard. Your wife Elizabeth will bear you a son, and you will name him John. You will have joy and gladness, and many will rejoice at his birth, for he will be great in the sight of the Lord. He must never drink wine or strong drink; even before his birth he will be filled with the Holy Spirit. He will turn many of the people of Israel to the Lord their God. With the spirit and power of Elijah he will go before him, to turn the hearts of *fathers to their children*, and the disobedient to the wisdom of the righteous, to make ready a people prepared for the Lord."

Reflection

Continue:

This passage is the prophecy of the angel about John the Baptist. It contains an interesting phrase. The angel says to Zechariah that his son will be like the Old Testament prophet Elijah in that he will "turn the hearts of fathers to their children". The angel is pointing to the fact that something is lacking in the relationship between fathers and their children, and that children need their fathers to turn their hearts toward them, or reconcile with them again.

Interestingly, the angel does *not* say that mothers need to be reconciled with their children. The words of the angel lead us to believe that the father-child relationship is more fragile and in need of healing than the mother-child relationship.

Just as fathers needed to be reconciled with their children in the time of Zechariah and his son John, so do they today. The world is filled with disheartening stories of fathers and their damaging relationships or lack of relationships with their children. In general, the father-son relationship is one of the most damaged of all. The overarching aim of this program is to begin to correct this trend by promoting, healing and strengthening the bond between the fathers and sons in this room.

Opening Prayer

Ask all to stand. Lead the following prayer:

Jesus,

please be with us during our time together.

Heal any rifts between father and son,

and turn their hearts towards each other.

Help these fathers and sons deepen their

love for one another and strengthen the bond between them.

We make this prayer in your name.

Amen.

Small Group Surveys

(about 20 minutes)

Pass out pens and index cards to each person. Direct the fathers to meet in one room with one of the facilitators and the sons to meet in another room with the other facilitator. Each facilitator leads a survey and sharing based on some main themes of the program using the following directions.

Survey and Sharing Directions for Fathers

1. Begin by reading the following reflection entitled "What Do I Want for My Son?" by Chaim Potok:

    Lord God, Master of the Universe, blest me with a brilliant son. And he cursed me with all the problems of raising him. Ah, what it is to have a brilliant son! Not a smart son, Lord, but a brilliant son! Joshua, a boy with a mind like a jewel. Ah, what a curse it is, what an anguish it is to have a son whose mind is like a pearl, like a sun.

    Lord, when my Joshua was six years old, I saw him reading a story, he swallowed it as one swallows food or water. There was no heart in my Joshua, there was only his mind. He was a mind in a body without a heart. It was a story about a poor old man and his struggle to get to Jerusalem before he died. Ah, how that man suffered! And my Joshua enjoyed the story, he enjoyed the last terrible page because when he finished it he realised for the first time what a splendid memory he possessed. He looked at me proudly and re-told the story from memory, and I cried inside my heart.

    I went outside and shouted to the Master of the Universe, "Why? What have you done to me? A mind like this I need for a son? A heart I need for my son. A soul I need for my son. Righteousness, mercy, strength to suffer and carry pain; that I want for my son, not a mind without a soul, without a heart."[7]

2. Allow a brief time for reflection. Then read the following questions. Between each question, pause so that the fathers can write their responses on their cards. Tell them to write one-word or short-phrase responses on the cards in the order the questions are read.

    ### Questions

    — What do you or did you like doing with your son?

    — What is one source of conflict you have with your son?

    — What is one incident of violence that has affected you, your family, or your neighbourhood?

- What is one word you associate with friendship?

- What hopes do you have for your son's life?

3. Ask the fathers to mark any responses they would be willing to personally share with the group. Ask the fathers to arrange their chairs in small group circles. (Limit the size of each group to eight persons. If there are more than eight fathers present, divide into equal sharing groups.) Designate one person to begin sharing. Ask him to introduce himself and share his response to one of the questions. Continue the process until every father has introduced himself and shared. (It is all right if someone does not wish to share any response. However, do ask that each person introduce himself to the group.) If there is time, go around the circles again, allowing each father to share his response to a second question.

4. Collect and shuffle the index cards from the fathers. Move back to the large meeting space.

Son Survey and Sharing Directions

1. Begin by reading the following words from Mark Twain:

    When I was 14 years old, I thought my father was an old ignoramus. When I became 21, I was surprised at how much the old man had learned in seven years.

2. Allow a brief time for reflection. Then read the following questions. Between each question, pause so that the teenagers can write their responses on their cards. Tell them to write one-word or short-phrase responses on the cards in the order the questions are called.

    ### Questions

    - What do you or did you like doing with your father?

    - What is one source of conflict you have with your father?

    - What is one incident of violence that has affected you, your family, or your neighbourhood?

    - What is one word you associate with friendship?

    - What hopes do you have for your life?

3. Ask the teens to mark any responses they would be willing to personally share with the group. Ask the teens to gather their chairs in small group circles. (Limit the size of each group to eight persons. If there are more than eight teens present, divide them into equal sharing groups.) Designate one person to begin sharing. Ask him to introduce himself and share his response to one of the questions. Continue the process until every son has introduced himself and shared. (It is all right if someone does not wish to share any response. However, do ask that each person introduce himself to the group.) If there is time, go around the circles again, allowing each teen to share his response to a second question.

4. Collect and shuffle the index cards from the sons. Report back to the large meeting space.

Survey Roundup

(about 10 minutes)

When everyone has returned, place the cards in two piles, designating one the *father* pile, the other the *son* pile. The two facilitators alternately read from the two piles of cards as a means of helping the group understand the important issues and experiences that fathers and sons share. Focus first on the responses to the first question, next on the responses to the second question and so on. Don't offer any comment on what you read. And don't read everything from any card because it will take too long and it is only one person's response. A broad representation of responses is needed to give an overview.

Father and Son Sharing

(about 10 minutes)

Advise the participants that part of the program involves one-to-one dialogue between fathers and sons. Ask each father and son to meet briefly to share and explain the responses they marked on their index cards. Write the following list of questions on the board for reference:

- What do you or did you like doing together?
- What is one source of conflict you have?
- What is one incident of violence that has affected you, your family, or your neighbourhood?
- What is one word you associate with friendship?
- What hopes do you have for your (son's) life?

Overview of Program

(about 15 minutes)

Take the participants through an overview of the six sessions of the program. Each of the questions from the father and son sharing relates to a major theme in the first five sessions. Refer to the questions as you give the presentation from the following script.

Presentation Script

During the course of the next few weeks, you will be attending six sessions that will help you to think more about the issues that arise from the five questions you just answered. I would like to offer a brief preview of each of the sessions.

The Father and Son Bond (Write on the board next to the first question.) The first session of the program looks at the father and son relationship. Doing things together is one part of that relationship. Some of you mentioned that you liked to kick the footy or go on camping trips together (mention other things from the cards). But this relationship, or bond, involves more. It involves learning about what each of you feels is important for life—your values. You can learn these things from talking with one another and observing one another in a variety of situations. For sons, this is an especially important task. Knowing your father well and developing a strong relationship with him is an essential part of growing into manhood.

Becoming a Man (Write on the board next to the second question.) As you know, a person goes through several physical and emotional changes in the teenage years. Changes in the way teenagers perceive God and religion also are dramatically affected. While there is no absolute definition of the kind of men you are or the kind of men you are becoming, one psychological theory has named four different archetypes of men—father, warrior, seeker, and sage—as a way to help you get a handle on why you think, feel, act, and believe as you do. Also, if a father and son are of different archetypes, the difference may be a source of conflict. This session will help you understand yourselves and each other better.

Dealing with Anger (Write on the board next to the third question.) Of the total prison population in this country, what percentage of prisoners would you estimate are men? (Allow one or two volunteers to offer suggestions.) Statistics show that women make up less than 10 per cent of the total prison population. Men are the great majority. Many of these men are in prison for committing violent crimes; in fact men are 20 times more likely to commit a violent crime than women. This session looks at the feeling of anger and some healthy ways to channel and control this feeling.

Friendships with Girls and Women (Write on the board next to the fourth question.) If you know about friendship, then you know about respect. To respect a friend means that you care about the person's safety and well-being. Respect is associated with freedom. You wouldn't force a friend to do something that he wouldn't want to do. All of you probably have close male friends. This session helps fathers communicate to their sons the importance of developing friendships with males *and* females. Friendships with young women are the foundation for a committed marriage. Friendships with one or two women can help to build respect for all women.

The Quest for Identity (Write on the board next to the fifth question.) A developmental task adolescents face is attaining a consistent sense of identity. Identity means who you are as a person. A good relationship between parents and children helps to this end. Also, your relationship to and service of God helps you to discover your ultimate identity, the vocation for life that God intends for you. This session will help you to look at your past and present for clues to how you can achieve everything you hope for, for yourself or for your son.

The Blessing Ritual (Write on the board.) The final session concludes with a blessing and a party. Everybody needs to be noticed, affirmed, admired, and delighted in. This form of validation of you and your life is called a blessing. This ritual will be followed by food, drink, and lots of reminiscing of the times we have shared with one another.

Allow for questions from the participants on any of the topics or process involved in the program.

Personal Talks

Continue, explaining the need for openness in sharing with others, between fathers and sons, and for prepared presentations by some fathers and some sons. Say:

The success of the program depends on your willingness to be honest and open with yourself, with your father or son, and with others in the group. Before the next session, pray for this grace, especially if you are not used to sharing personal stories, feelings and values with others.

Also, for four of the sessions, we will ask volunteers among the fathers and sons to prepare personal presentations on topics related to the session's theme. Your willingness to give one of these presentations is much appreciated! The talks are short—five to 10 minutes—and involve reflecting on a series of sentence starters or questions that we will provide you. You only need to share one or two of your reflections with the group. For the first session, we would like to hear from two fathers about the relationships they had as teenagers with their own fathers. I'd ask all the fathers to consider helping this way. At the end of the meeting, please see me if you are interested, and I will give you a paper that will help you prepare. Thank you!

Program Announcements

(about 10 minutes)

Continue in the large meeting room. The program coordinator returns to make some announcements concerning business and housekeeping issues in the program. Add, eliminate, or adapt these issues to fit the specific requirements of your program.

Venue

Make sure the participants know where to meet for Session One.

Timetable

Pass out a schedule of times and dates for all six sessions, Resource 1, "Father and Son Program Timetable."

Cost

Inform the participants of the cost of the program, if any.

Father and Son Information Sheets

Pass out the appropriate halves of Resource 2 to the fathers and sons. Ask them to fill out the information and return the sheets to you. Provide pens or pencils if necessary.

Casual Meals

Explain the procedure of the casual meals (time and place). Ask the fathers (with sons) to sign up on the sheet (Resource 3) to provide a dish of food. Make sure to specify how many servings of each salad, main course or dessert that each is expected to provide.

Personal Talk Reminder

Remind and encourage fathers to volunteer for the first talks to be given in Session One. Tell them to see the facilitators at the end of the meeting to pick up Resource 4, "The Father and Son Bond."

Grandfathers

A group of fathers and sons may be in the fortunate situation of being able to include one or two grandfathers in the program. Say:

We would like you to consider the possibility of inviting your grandfathers to join in this fathers and sons program. This could be either your son's maternal or paternal grandfather. The inclusion of one or two grandfathers adds an important generational dimension to the program. Often there is a very deep bond between grandfather and grandson that we would like to celebrate in the program.

Conclusion

(about 5 minutes)

Prayer

Ask everyone to stand. Lead a recitation of the *Our Father*.

Resource Table

Remind the fathers and sons of the date of the next session. Dismiss the group but remain available with the facilitators at a resource table to answer questions about the program, collect father and son information sheets, take casual meal sign ups, and meet with fathers who wish to volunteer for the personal talks for Session One.

Session One

The Father & Son Bond

Background Information for Facilitators

A healthy family is built on a foundation of love, trust, respect and communication among its members. When any of these elements is lacking or absent, the basic structure of the family is on shaky ground. One purpose of this session is to recognise the importance of these basic elements of the family unit and to add to and build upon them with respect to the relationship between adolescent sons and their fathers. For many, this will seem an arduous task. Communication between fathers and adolescent sons may be at a standstill; some fathers and sons go weeks or months without exchanging anything other than basic civilities. As an adolescent "spreads his wings" and gains new freedom, fathers often feel overwhelmed by the choices at their sons' disposal and fearful of or threatened by the possibility that their sons will make negative choices. Yet the love between a father and son usually does not waver even in the midst of this difficult time. For example, fathers are still very concerned about their sons' safety and well-being; adolescents feel the same about their fathers.

This session helps to reopen or build up the lines of communication between sons and fathers, and by doing so, to reinforce the trust and respect they have for one another. This is an important task that also has spiritual ramifications. Jesus often addresses God as a loving "Abba", or "Daddy". The parable of the lost son highlights the love and care of a father for his two sons. Without day-to-day experience of a father's love, a son may have difficulty understanding the unfathomable love that God has for each one of us. One of the goals of this session, and the program as a whole, is to help sons to see their fathers as men of faith and as models of a God who loves them without bounds.

Pastoral Responses

The purpose of this session is to:

- provide an opportunity for fathers and sons to evaluate their relationship and identify its strengths and weaknesses;
- help fathers and sons build on their relationship with trust.

Supply List

For this session, you will need:

- name tags
- scrap paper
- a supply of pens or pencils
- (optional) a recording of ocean water sound effects
- (optional) CD player
- copies of Resource 5, "Personal Reflection: The Father and Son Bond"
- copies of Resource 6, "Guidelines for Small Group Sharing"
- copies of Resource 7, "Session 1 Small Group Sharing Questions"

- supply of writing and drawing paper
- small slips of paper

Session Outline

Welcome and Meal Sharing (about 45 minutes)

Pledges, Expectations, and Introductions (about 30 minutes)

Gospel Reading (about 15 minutes)

Thinking About Your Father (about 50 minutes)

Small Group Sharing (about 30 minutes)

Summary and Conclusion (about 10 minutes)

Welcome and Meal Sharing

(about 45 minutes)

Casual Meal

Set up tables with nine chairs at each to allow small groups (ideally four fathers, four sons, and one moderator) to eat together. Place a name tag near each place-setting so that the participants can identify their seats. This will allow them to begin to get to know the members of their small groups, which will remain the same throughout the program.

Conduct the meal buffet-style or in any way that works well for your group.

Offer a formal welcome to the participants and grace before the meal. Then allow the participants to socialise informally until it is time to begin the session. If you would like to have one group act out the gospel reading, choose a group now so that they can eat quickly and have time to prepare before the session starts (see pages 33-34).

Give a 10-minute warning near the end of the mealtime. Ask the participants to clear their tables and move to the large meeting room for the beginning of the session.

Pledges, Expectations and Introductions

(about 30 minutes)

When everyone is seated, go over the expectations you have for the program. Say:

Welcome to the first session of the *Between Fathers and Sons* program. We hope it will be a rewarding experience for you. We do have some basic expectations that we feel will enhance this program for you.

First, we ask that you attend each session. Your absence changes the dynamic of the group and creates a gap in the continuity of the program. Your presence is invaluable to the success of the program. As you noticed, your seats were assigned during our casual meal. The people who were at your table will meet with you for small group sharing throughout the program. Also, punctuality is important. Please plan to arrive as close to the start of the mealtime as possible.

Sharing is at the heart of the program. Your openness, courage, and generosity in sharing personally will make the lessons of these sessions much more meaningful. We will go over some guidelines for small-group sharing later on. For now, know that the confidentiality of what is shared will be respected. Please make note of these standards of confidentiality:

Standards of Confidentiality

— In our role as facilitators, we pledge to keep the confidence of the participants by not repeating any personal stories we hear shared during the program.

— Likewise, we ask you not to break confidences by repeating anything you hear shared in small group discussions or before the entire group.

Trust Exercise

Ask all the participants to stand, the fathers near their sons. Say:

Trust is an essential element of any good relationship. Trust means the "placement of confidence". For the purposes of this group, trust is absolutely necessary so that we have the freedom to grow by honestly examining and sharing our past and present experiences and our hopes for the future. Trust is also a crucial part of a relationship between a father and a son for the same reasons. Let's do an exercise to witness the trust you have for one another.

Demonstrate the exercise with the other facilitator: Face away from the facilitator with your back toward his hands. Fold your arms and close your eyes. With your legs locked and straight, rock back on your heels and let yourself fall backward as your partner catches you.

After the demonstration, ask the fathers and sons to find a clear space and do the exercise themselves, the fathers "catching" the sons.

Allow a few minutes for everyone to try. Then tell the participants to sit down. Call on one father and son pair to reverse roles with the son catching the father as a demonstration for the entire group. (Choose a son who is physically able to catch his father!)

Offer these words in conclusion. Say:

When we say something very personal to someone else, it's as though we are free-falling. When the other person responds affirmatively by listening, saying something constructive, or not breaking our confidence, they "catch" us, we experience trust. In this program, we are working to establish relationships, particularly between fathers and sons, in which trust is an essential and accepted element.

Introductions

Write the following on the board:

What is/are:

- Your name.
- Your school/occupation.

- The most interesting thing that happened to you in the past 24 hours.
- Your expectations for the program.

Then, say:

When I am finished giving directions, I will ask you to move around the room and interview one person, asking him for answers to the questions on the board. You cannot interview your own father or your own son. Also, two teenagers cannot interview each other or two adults cannot interview each other. If you don't think you can remember the information you are given, take a piece of scrap paper and write it down. You will be asked to share the results of the interview with the whole group. Any questions? (Pause.) Let's begin.

Allow about 10 minutes for the interviews. Then ask everyone to sit in the large meeting area. Randomly choose one interview pair to stand before the group and introduce each other, sharing the information they learned. Then ask all of the interview pairs in turn to introduce each other. Write key words on the board or on butcher paper to summarise the expectations the participants have for the program. Repeat the process until everyone has been introduced. At the end of the session, transcribe the list for your own information and to help facilitate an evaluation of the program in Session Six (see page 83).

Optional: If the group is too large, conduct this exercise in the pre-assigned small groups.

Gospel Reading

(about 45 minutes)

Luke 15:11-32

Introduce and read the parable of the father and the lost son. If possible, share the parable in your own words or present it as a dramatic reading with the other facilitator. You might also consider asking one of the small groups to present it as a short skit. They can follow this script:

Then Jesus said, There was a man who had two sons. The younger of them said to his father, "Father, give me the share of the property that will belong to me." So he divided his property between them. A few days later the younger son gathered all he had and traveled to a distant country, and there he squandered his property in dissolute living.

When he had spent everything, a severe famine took place throughout that country, and he began to be in need. So he went and hired himself out to one of the citizens of that country, who sent him to his fields to feed the pigs. He would gladly have filled himself with the pods that the pigs were eating; and no one gave him anything. But when he came to himself he said, "How many of my father's hired hands have bread enough and to spare, but here I am dying of hunger! I will get up and go to my father, and I will say to him, 'Father, I have sinned against heaven and before you; I am no longer worthy to be called your son; treat me like one of your hired hands'." So he set off and went to his father.

But while he was still far off, his father saw him and was filled with compassion; he ran and put his arms around him and kissed him. Then the son said to him, "Father, I have sinned against heaven and before you; I am no longer worthy to be called your son." But the father said to his slaves, "Quickly, bring out a robe—the best one—and put it on him; put a ring on his finger and sandals on his feet. And get the fatted calf and kill it, and let us eat and celebrate; for this son of mine was dead and is alive again; he was lost and is found!" And they began to celebrate.

Now his elder son was in the field; and when he came and approached the house, he heard music and dancing. He called one of the slaves and asked what was going on. He replied, "Your brother has come, and your father has killed the fatted calf, because he has got him back safe and sound." Then he became angry and refused to go in. His father came out and began to plead with him. But he answered his father, "Listen! For all these years I have been working like a slave for you, and I have never disobeyed your command; yet you have never given me even a young goat so that I might celebrate with my friends. But when this son of yours came back, who has devoured your property with prostitutes, you killed the fatted calf for him!"

Then the father said to him, "Son, you are always with me, and all that is mine is yours. But we had to celebrate and rejoice, because this brother of yours was dead and has come to life; he was lost and has been found."

Reflection

Continue:

In this parable, we hear about two sons. Each has a different kind of relationship with his father. *Both* have problems with their father. The younger son tests his father's love. He takes his inheritance, leaves home, and fails miserably. Surprisingly, his failed attempt to make a life of his own eventually promotes growth in his relationship with his father.

Think about your own life. Can you think of a time when facing the truth about your weaknesses strengthened your relationship with your father?

The older son doesn't leave home. He plays it safe and ultimately doesn't seem to grow in a positive way. Even though he was always physically near to his father, the last we hear from him is that he is emotionally and spiritually far away.

Think about your relationship with your father or your son. How are you far away from one another? How are you close to one another? How do you envision your relationship with your son or your father in the future? Will it be more like the relationship of the younger son with his father? Or more like the relationship of the older son with his dad? How so?

Prayer

Ask all to bow their heads in prayer. Say:

Jesus, in the parable of the father and his two sons,

you show us the depths of a father's love, the depths of God's love for us.

Please be with us during our time together.

Aid the healing of any divisions and hurts between the fathers and sons in this group.

Deepen our understanding of your Abba-Father's love for us,

and help our trust in you to grow deeper.

We ask this in your name.

Amen.

Thinking About Your Father

(about 50 minutes)

Ask the participants to be seated. Continue with a presentation on the theme of trust between a father and son, and its correlation in the trust God has for us and we have for God. Tell this story in your own words:

There was a group of botanists exploring the Amazon region for new species of plants. One of the botanists was surveying the forest through binoculars when he spied a plant that had the most beautiful and unique flower he had ever seen. Unfortunately the plant was down in a deep ravine with steep cliffs on either side of it. He and his colleagues realised that to collect a sample of the plant would mean that one of them would have to be lowered by rope down into the ravine, a very dangerous proposition.

There were some boys from one of the indigenous tribes of the area who had been watching them work, and one of the scientists suggested to the others that they pay one of the boys to be lowered down by rope and collect the plant. They all agreed.

They put this proposal to one of the boys who looked at them and then looked down into the depths of the ravine. The boy said, "I will do what you ask, but could you wait an hour?" They agreed and the boy went off.

About an hour later, the boy returned with an older man from his tribe. The boy said, "I am prepared to be lowered down the cliff if this man holds the rope. He is my father."

The sense of confidence the boy had in his father was such that he felt he could trust his father with his very life. Many of you may feel this same sense of trust for your father or from your son. If so, this is a great gift. This gift of trust is the same offer of the father to the younger son in the parable we heard. It is the same trust that God offers to each of us: I will be your God. I will always love you. I will never let you go. When the relationship between a father and a son is built on this kind of trust, it models the relationship God seeks with us.

The Father and Son Bond: Stories of Two Fathers

Introduce the two fathers who have prepared talks based on Resource 4. Build on the theme of trust in your introduction. Say:

Now we have the privilege of hearing from two fathers of their relationships with their fathers, how trust played a part in it, and how their fathers have influenced their lives.

Ask one father to begin, allowing him approximately five minutes to speak. Then call on the other to give a five-minute presentation.

Thank both fathers and ask the participants for a few positive comments on what was shared. Elicit the comments with a few well-phrased questions. For example: "Did anyone hear anything familiar in these two talks? What was the most encouraging thing you heard?"

Imagination Exercise: Who Is Your Father?

Dim the lights in the room. Tell the participants you will be conducting an imagination exercise. Ask them to sit straight in their chairs without straining and put their feet flat on the floor. Tell them to shut their eyes and to breathe slowly and deeply. Begin playing a recording of ocean sounds (optional). Read the following imagination story slowly and clearly, pausing between sentences and a bit longer after the questions:

Imagine yourself walking alone along an isolated stretch of beach. As you walk along, you feel the sand under your bare feet. Every now and then a small wave laps over your feet. The water is cool and refreshing. A slight breeze is blowing. You hear a seagull call and the waves returning to sea.

Up ahead you see a figure in the distance walking toward you. As you get closer, you have a peculiar experience. You recognise that it is your father.

How do you feel as you walk toward your father? What is the look on his face? As you come closer and closer together, you notice he is holding something in his hands. What is it? You remember that you too are holding something in your hands. What are you holding?

You stand facing each other. What do you both say? What do you both do? Is there any connection between the object you are holding and the object he is holding? What is the connection?

Continue playing the recording of ocean sounds or allow a time of silence.

Personal Reflection

Pass out copies of Resource 5, "Personal Reflection: The Father and Son Bond". Read the directions and explain each of the listed exercises. Tell the participants that they will be asked to share what they write only with their own father or son. Allow about 10 minutes for individual reflection and writing.

Father and Son Dialogue

Ask the father and son pairs to move together for "one-to-one" sharing. Invite them to share for about 10 minutes from the Personal Reflection resource using this format:

- One person tells which reflection exercise he chose and then shares what he wrote or drew. The other person asks clarifying questions or offers a personal response to the reflection.

- The process is repeated, with the second person beginning.

- As time allows, the father and son share any other comments, questions, or insights about the material presented to this point in the session.

Small Group Sharing

(about 30 minutes)

Distribute copies of Resource 6, "Guidelines for Small Group Sharing" to the participants and read them out so that all are aware of the expectations. Tell the participants that they will be meeting with their small groups (as per the pre-session casual meal) and sharing their responses to some questions related to this session. Go over the guidelines. Then pass out a copy of the "Session 1 Small Group Sharing Questions" (Resource 7) to each participant. Direct the groups to separate areas. Tell them they will have about 25 minutes for sharing.

(As it is the first session, you may suggest that the group members reintroduce themselves before they begin the discussion.)

Summary and Conclusion

(about 10 minutes)

Call the participants back to the large meeting area. Give each person two slips of paper. Tell them to use one slip to write one sentence on something they liked about the session, the other to write one sentence on something they disliked. Have them put a plus (+) on the first strip and a minus (-) on the second. Allow about five minutes for writing. Then, say:

I encourage you to sign your names on your slips, but you do not have to.

Collect the slips and use them as an evaluation tool for Session One, and to help in your preparation for the following sessions.

Concluding Prayer

Choose one or two verses from Luke 15:11-24 to read as part of a final prayer; for example: "My son, you are with me always and all I have is yours." Repeat the verse(s) four or five times, meditatively, pausing between each reading. Then ask everyone to stand and join in praying the *Our Father*.

Reminders

Remind the fathers and sons responsible for the casual meal dishes to bring them for Session Two. Remind everyone of the date and time of Session Two. Thank them for their attendance and dismiss them on time.

Session Two

Becoming a Man

Background Information for Facilitators

As with any understanding of human development, the notion of "becoming a man" is one that should be examined on many levels. The intent of this session is to help the fathers and sons touch on some of the kinds of development occurring during adolescence and to explore how this development impacts the lives of the teenagers and their relationship with their fathers, now and in the future. Several categories of growth that take place in adolescence are listed during the session.

The particular focus of Session Two, however, is an explanation of *four male archetypes*. These are descriptions of four models of male psychological behaviour: father, seeker, warrior and sage. The archetypes provide a foundation for understanding individual male behaviours and the dynamics of relationships between fathers and sons who may be of differing archetypes. The archetypes presented in this session were developed by Tad Guzie and Noreen Monroe Guzie in their book *About Men and Women*. (It would be very helpful, though not essential, for you to read the Guzies' book in preparation for this session.)

Often overlooked in the process of becoming a man is an adolescent's changing religious development and imaging of God. A shift in religious thinking usually occurs during adolescence, paralleling the identity crisis typical of this period. Early adolescence is a time of peer-orientation and self-doubt. It is also the beginning of independent thinking and introspection. Adolescents in the 13 to 15-year-old range are in the process of developing an entirely new spiritual outlook, though they may for the most part seem uninterested in faith or apathetic. Later adolescence is marked by questioning and searching faith. Teens at this age are very adept at articulating questions and doubts as well as their convictions and commitments. An imagination exercise helps teens and adults alike to clarify their images of God.

Pastoral Responses

The purpose of this session is to:

- examine some of the changes that mark "becoming a man";
- define four male archetypes and help the fathers and sons recognise patterns of their own behaviour in one or more of these models;
- help fathers and sons understand how differences in archetypes can cause difficulties in their relationships;
- call attention to the changing ways that adolescents visualise God.

Supply List

For this session, you will need:

- name tags;
- a supply of pens or pencils;
- index cards;
- multiple copies of Resource 8, "Understanding Archetypes" (one for each participant) copies of Resource 9, "Personality Profile" (one for each participant);

- copies of Resource 10, "The Four Male Archetypes" (one for each participant);
- (optional) recording of instrumental reflective music;
- (optional) CD player;
- copies of Resource 6, "Guidelines for Small Group Sharing";
- copies of Resource 11, "Session 2 Small Groups Sharing Questions";
- small slips of paper;
- four copies of Resource 12, "Dealing with Anger".

Session Outline

Welcome and Meal Sharing (about 45 minutes)

Introduction and Gospel Reading (about 15 minutes)

What Does It Mean to Be A Man? (about 50 minutes)

Searching for God (about 15 minutes)

Small Group Sharing (about 40 minutes)

Summary and Conclusion (about 15 minutes)

Welcome and Meal Sharing

(about 45 minutes)

Casual Meal

Arrange the room with tables for open seating. As the participants arrive, pass out name tags. Encourage the father and son pairs to sit with people who are not in their regular small sharing groups so that they are able meet and socialise with as many people in the program as possible.

Conduct the meal buffet-style or in any way that works well for your group.

Offer a formal welcome to the participants and say grace before the meal. Allow the participants to socialise informally during the meal until it is time to begin the session.

Give a 10-minute warning near the end of the mealtime. Ask the participants to clean up their tables and move to the large meeting room for the beginning of the session.

Introduction and Gospel Reading

(about 15 minutes)

After everyone is settled, introduce the topic. Say:

The title of this session is "Becoming a Man". Each of the words in the title is an important one. "Becoming" is important because it signifies a process that is ongoing. In earlier times, boys did become men literally overnight; for example, when their fathers took them from home to work. Today, a period of adolescence marks a longer time of change and development. Some of these changes are easy to see; for example, puberty is a time when a boy physically matures. But even puberty isn't an instantaneous change; it can last over a number of months or even years. The word "a" also has meaning. Note that the title of the session is not "Becoming the Man". "A" is the better word because it recognises how God intends all men to be individuals, different from one another and not turned out like products on an assembly line. Finally, the word "man" is used to signify both a particular gender (malehood) and a stage of development (adulthood). Being a man is different from being a woman or being a boy. This session will cover some, though not all, of the dynamics necessary to becoming a man.

Luke 2:41-50

Continue. Say:

Part of what is involved in becoming a man is a search for God. In discovering more about who God is, we discover more of who we are. This searching is common among teenagers; in fact, the one story about the adolescent Jesus recorded in the Bible addresses this need to strike out on one's own and discover who God is and what God wants for one's life.

Present the story of the 12-year-old Jesus being found by Mary and Joseph in the temple. If possible, tell the story in your own words or read it in parts with the other facilitator:

Now every year his parents went to Jerusalem for the festival of the Passover. And when he was 12 years old, they went up as usual for the festival. When the festival was ended and they started to return, the boy Jesus stayed behind in Jerusalem, but his parents did not know it. Assuming that he was in the group of travellers, they went a day's journey. Then they started to look for him among their relatives and friends. When they did not find him, they returned to Jerusalem to search for him.

After three days they found him in the temple, sitting among the teachers, listening to them and asking them questions. And all who heard him were amazed at his understanding and his answers. When his parents saw him, they were astonished; and his mother said to him, "Child, why have you treated us like this? Look, your father and I have been searching for you in great anxiety." He said to them, "Why were you searching for me? Did you not know that I must be in my Father's house?" But they did not understand what he said to them.

Then he went down with them and came to Nazareth, and was obedient to them.

Reflection: The Search for God During Adolescence

Continue:

The story is unique—the only one we have of Jesus' adolescence. And it shows us a pretty typical picture of adolescence: Jesus and his parents don't seem to understand each other very well. Joseph and Mary think Jesus is being disobedient and behaving dangerously. Jesus doesn't understand what they are so worried about; he's fine. He's been in the Temple all the time. Didn't they *know* that's where he'd be?

Do you think you fathers and sons could do any better? Imagine you and your family take a trip to a big city you don't live in. Now, Mary and Joseph didn't know Jesus was missing for a whole day, which seems unlikely to us. But they were travelling with a large group, mostly extended family members. So Mary and Joseph assumed Jesus was with some of his cousins, aunts or uncles. Only when night came did they really start their search.

Parents today would likely know in a much shorter period of time—probably within hours—if their son was separated from them. Imagine a situation when a separation like this could take place. (Pass out index cards.) Sons, write three places you would go if you were separated from your parents for a few hours in a big city. Fathers, on your cards, write the first three places you would look for your son in a big city. (Allow a few minutes for writing.)

Now share your responses with one another. (Pause.) Raise your hands if you matched all three responses. (Acknowledge any participants who matched all three responses.) Actually, fathers who can match any of their responses with their sons' should feel pretty good. Are there any fathers who wouldn't have found their sons in any of the places they'd have looked? (Check responses.) In any case, you can imagine how Joseph felt when he walked in the temple after three days of searching for his son. Surely he had looked in all the "logical" places for an adolescent boy; today he would probably have started with the police station or the hospital. Mary and Joseph's worry and anxiety were, and are, perfectly normal parental responses.

But Jesus' surprise at his parent's concern is also normal. As an adolescent boy, he is beginning to say to his parents: "Stop worrying about me all the time. Let me take care of myself. Let me do things my way. I can't live under your control forever." Although this is not a clean break, and Jesus does return to Nazareth with his parents and live under their authority, he does test the boundaries of family life in this story. He is moving beyond his parents' control and protection for at least short periods of time. And a key element of this exploring is his spiritual quest. Jesus must uncover his own personal relationship with God.

Like Jesus, the sons in this room must test their family boundaries and gradually move beyond the control and protection of their mothers and fathers. They too must uncover who God is for them, their own personal experience of God. And they must expect some reluctance from their parents as Jesus faced from Mary and Joseph.

What Does It Mean to Be A Man?

(about 50 minutes)

Continue in the large meeting area with a presentation that encourages the participants to identify the factors that separate men from boys. As you record their answers on the board, try to group them logically. Say:

Let's see how many changes we can identify that occur as boys become men. There are two I can think of right off: Their **voices change** (write on board) and they learn to **drive a car** (write). What else happens?

Continue to solicit and suggest responses until you have two or more examples from each of the following categories (use as headings for the examples):

- **chronological growth;**
- **physical growth;**
- **mental growth;**
- **social growth;**
- **spiritual growth.**

Continue:

Taken together, the factors listed here give us a good clue as to what is involved in becoming a man. However, many or all of these factors are future-oriented. All vary greatly from person to person. For example, some males go through puberty in their early teens, others in their middle or late teens. Another factor that can help us to know what it means to become and be a man is based on deep personality traits that have been present from the beginning of our lives. This factor has to do with our **psychological makeup**.

Large Group Sharing

Tell the group about one unique character or personality trait your parents have told you that you have possessed from infancy (e.g., compassion, stubbornness, loquacity, timidity, etc.). Try to offer examples of how you manifested this trait as a child and as an adult. Then, address a question to the fathers. Say:

Let's take a show of hands. Does your son exhibit at least one personality or character trait today that he had as an infant? (Pause.) This is evidence that we are born with a basic psychological makeup.

Distribute photocopies of the Resource 8, "Understanding Archetypes". Then continue from the script.

Script (continued)

The human mind is something like an iceberg. Just as 90 per cent of an iceberg is out of sight under water, so too we are unaware of much of what is contained in our mind. At this moment, you are listening to me with the conscious part of your mind. That is like the 10 per cent of the iceberg that is above the water level. But as you can imagine from the drawing, there are vast areas of the human mind of which we are *unconscious*. When we are asleep, the unconscious mind shows itself in the images we have in our dreams.

The *collective unconscious* is the deepest level of the human mind. Stored at this level are the basic components of our psychological makeup, present from the time of our birth. Psychologists have studied these components and have developed psychological profiles based on them. Psychologists Tad Guzie and Noreen Monroe Guzie have named basic psychological components—*archetypes*—for both men and women. We will look closely at the four archetypes for men—*father*, *seeker*, *warrior*, and *sage*—and help you to name the primary archetype out of which you act.

Knowing and naming your archetype is helpful because it can enable you to see some of the behaviours and patterns of manhood you may be psychologically conditioned to act out. Also, fathers and sons who act from different archetypes may have problems understanding each other. Knowing and naming your archetypes can help you resolve some of the problems that may arise from having different archetypes.

Survey

Pass out copies of Resource 9, "Personality Profile", and pens to each person. Read the directions. Allow about five minutes for individual marking of the profile. Next, tell the participants to follow along from the chart at the bottom of Resource 9 as you describe each of the archetypes from the script. Pause after each archetype to allow participants to tally their responses.

Script (continued)

A man with a **father** archetype finds his identity in providing for and protecting others. The father likes to care for others. You don't have to ever have children of your own to have this archetype. The father is not concerned with power for its own sake. Rather he uses his power to protect his brood—family, friendship group, employees—from anything threatening. The father enjoys being with his "family". The father is the guardian of tradition and convention. He values stability, permanence, and the status quo. He wants to pass on to others what has worked well for him. Naturally conservative, he thinks, "What has helped me in the past will help you now."

Look at your personality profile. Numbers **1**, **5**, **9**, and **13** describe characteristics of the father archetype. Tally your responses to these four statements in the father section of the chart.

While the father is satisfied with "things as they have always been," the **seeker** wants to explore, to try new ways. He is often very creative. His life is one of searching and questing. He likes to do his own thing. While the father is concerned with the traditions of the group—family, organisations, religion, etc.—the seeker can feel stifled by them. The seeker acts as if rules don't apply to him. Instead, he develops his own set of rules that mostly protect his freedom to be a seeker. Negatively, the seeker can be irresponsible and may never grow up. At his best, he may "boldly go where no one has gone before".

Numbers **2**, **6**, **10**, and **14** describe characteristics of the seeker archetype. Tally your responses to statements 2, 6, 10, and 14 in the seeker section. For example, if you marked numbers 2 and 10 "V", number 6 "N" and number 14 "S" then you'll put two tally marks under the "V", one under the "N", and one under the "S".

A person with primarily a **warrior** archetype is one who sets goals and achieves them. The warrior enjoys competition and is not afraid of a struggle or a fight. Efficiency is his trademark.

The warrior's goals always come first. The warrior archetype is socially acceptable for a man in his 20s and 30s because he is meant to be a man with the drive to get things done. Because a warrior is energised by what is achievable, he often has little patience for people who live by values other than efficiency. He sometimes has trouble with relationships. For the warrior, the task comes first, relationships second.

Numbers **3**, **7**, **11**, and **15** describe characteristics of the warrior archetype. Tally your responses to these statements in the warrior section of the chart.

The **sage** is known as a thinker. He is constantly developing a coherent, personal philosophy of life that he thinks others need too. Therefore he is always attempting to articulate what he believes so that others will understand. For the sage "meaning" takes precedence over "doing", so even in a busy meeting where important decisions have to be made, or during a class where a paper has to be written, you may find the sage daydreaming to himself or philosophising to others. A sage often plays a vital role in the advancement of ideas and the improvement of society, but he may need more practical people to make his ideas work. Hence the description "absent minded professor" is often associated with the sage.

Numbers **4**, **8**, **12**, and **16** describe characteristics of the sage archetype. Tally your responses to these last statements in the sage section.

Optional: Pass out copies of Resource 10, "The Four Male Archetypes", to each person. Allow time for them to review the presentation and check their markings.

Your chart and these descriptions may give you some clue as to which is your dominant archetype. To score your archetype, assign two points for each tally in the "very much" column, one point for each tally in the "somewhat" column, and no points for each tally in the "not much" column. Add your points for each archetype and write them in the "total" column. Remember, people act out the characteristics of all the archetypes at various times. As you think about your primary archetype, consider how it may affect your relationships with others. Knowing that there are differences in the way people are "programmed" can help you to be tolerant and understanding of their words, actions, and behaviours. For our purposes, we want to focus on your relationship with your father or son and how similarities and differences in archetypes may affect it.

Individual Reflection

Write the following sentence starters on the board:

    I believe my primary archetype is . . .

    The characteristics I have of this archetype are . . .

    I believe my father's (son's) primary archetype is . . .

    The characteristics he has of this archetype are . . .

    I think the major difficulties in our relationship can be improved by . . .

    Understanding archetypes can help us improve our relationship by . . .

Tell the fathers and sons to work individually to finish each sentence on the back of Resource 10. Allow about 10 to 15 minutes for writing.

Father and Son Dialogue

Ask the father and son pairs to move into one-to-one sharing and dialogue about the presentation on archetypes. Tell them to use the sentence starters as openers for dialogue using this format:

- One person shares his first sentence. The second person comments on what was said; for example: "Though you have many characteristics of the warrior, I think you also tend to be a seeker, especially when you look for ways to do new things, like when we were repairing the car."

- The second person shares his first sentence, the first person comments. The process alternates in this way for all the sentence starters.

Allow about 10 minutes for this dialogue. Then call everyone back from their one-to-one sharing. Say, in summary:

Our psychological makeup and our archetypes are unique to us, part of God's creative action in making us who we are. Understanding how our archetypes affect and have affected us can help us in this ongoing process of "becoming a man".

Searching for God

(about 15 minutes)

Recall with the participants the gospel story of Jesus' search for God during his adolescence. Say:

We learn from Jesus that part of the process of becoming a man is the spiritual quest to experience God in a personal way. Please make yourselves comfortable for the next exercise. Put your feet flat on the floor. Sit straight without straining. Relax. Shut your eyes. Breathe slowly and deeply.

Read the following imagination exercise script, pausing briefly at the end of each sentence, a bit longer after a question. If possible, play a soft recording of instrumental music to accompany your reading.

Imagination Exercise Script

Imagine you are sitting on a mountain top overlooking a vast city. It is twilight, the sun has just set, and you notice the lights coming on in the great city. Watch them coming on until the whole city seems to be a lake of lights. You are sitting there all alone, gazing at this beautiful spectacle. What are you feeling?

After a while, you hear footsteps behind you and you know that they are the footsteps of a holy man who lives in these parts, a hermit. He looks at you gently and says just one sentence to you: "If you go down to the city tonight, you will find God." Having said this, he turns and walks away. No explanations, no time for further questions.

You have a feeling that this man knows what he is talking about. What do you feel like doing?

Do you feel like acting on his statement and going into the city? Or, would you rather stay where you are?

Whatever you feel, do go down into the city in search of God. What do you feel as you go down the mountain?

You have now come to the outskirts of the city and you have to decide where to go to search for God. Please follow the dictates of your heart in choosing the place you go to. Don't be guided by where you think you should go. Just go where your heart tells you to go. Where is this place?

What happens when you arrive there? What do you find there? What do you do there? What happens to you? Do you find God there? In what way? Or, are you disappointed in not finding God? What do you do then? Do you choose to go somewhere else? Or do you just stay where you are?

Wherever you are, whatever you are doing, stop for a moment and look around you. All around, appearing suddenly, out of nowhere, are dozens of images of God—dozens, hundreds, thousands. They look real, three-dimensional, as if you could reach out and touch them. But don't just yet.

First, look at them all. Many of them are familiar; someone has told you of them: the cross, a splash of water, the star of David, a breath of wind, a flame, the empty tomb, wheat and grapes, the faces of the poor. Look around some more and begin to consider what symbol of God speaks most clearly to you today. When you find it, reach out and take it reverently into your hands. Having chosen your symbol, consider it carefully. Give it your attention. What are you feeling as you gaze at this symbol? Say something to the symbol. Now imagine that it speaks back to you. What do you say? What does it say?

Become the symbol and look at yourself standing there reverently. What do you feel as you see yourself from this perspective? Now return to yourself standing there holding the symbol. Stay for a while in silent contemplation. Then bid farewell to your symbol, knowing that you can and will come back to it.

Allow a few minutes of silence or background music to conclude the exercise.

Small Group Sharing

(about 40 minutes)

Distribute copies of Resource 6, "Guidelines for Small Group Sharing", and review each of the guidelines. Tell the participants that they will be meeting with the same small group that formed at the first session. Pass out a copy of Resource 11, "Session 2 Small Group Sharing Questions", to each participant. Direct the groups to separate areas for the sharing. Read the directions. Tell them they will have about 40 minutes for sharing.

Summary and Conclusion

(about 15 minutes)

Call the participants back to the large meeting area. Give a small slip of paper to each person. Write a list of adjectives on the board (e.g., **surprised**, **inspired**, **helped**, **discouraged**, **bored**, **confused**, **impressed**). Tell the participants to use one of these adjectives or another of their own choosing to describe in a sentence how they feel about the content of this session. Signing the slip of paper is optional.

Allow about five minutes for writing. Collect the slips. Use them to help your evaluation of this session.

Session Three Preparations

Ask for two father and son pairs to prepare short talks for Session Three on the feeling of anger and ways to express anger. Tell them to see you at the conclusion of the session for more explanation and to take a copy of Resource 12, "Dealing with Anger". Also, ask *every* father and son pair to bring in one family photo or magazine photo depicting someone who is visibly angry.

Concluding Prayer

Ask everyone to stand. Extend your hands over the fathers and sons. Pray in these or similar words:

> Lord, thank you for our time together.
>
> Bless and keep each of us safe until we meet again.
>
> We ask this in your name.
>
> Amen.

Reminders

Remind the fathers and sons responsible for Casual items for Session Three to bring them. Remind everyone of the date and time of Session Three. Thank them for their attendance and dismiss them on time.

Session Three

Dealing with Anger

Background Information for Facilitators

Anger is an emotion. Like other emotions, anger is neither good nor bad of itself. Yet because many people express anger in violent ways, anger has come to be viewed as a negative emotion. Learning how to express anger in positive ways is a sign of healthy and productive living. Positive strategies in this area are especially important today for adolescent males.

Today, violence among this age group and gender is at dangerous proportions. In the past 30 years, juvenile arrest rates for violent crimes have increased by nearly 300 per cent. Arrest rates for males peak at age 16 and decline thereafter. Violence against oneself is also increasing among adolescents. Suicide is the second or third leading cause of death among teenagers in any given year (accidents are first; homicides are either second or third). From a developmental sense, these figures are not totally surprising: adolescence is a stage where males are attempting to prove themselves as men. Without positive male role models available to show productive ways of dealing with anger and channeling aggressive tendencies, the incidents and degrees of violence perpetrated by adolescents are likely to increase. Additionally, it is important to realise that violent crime is almost exclusively a male problem. As mentioned earlier, males make up over 90 per cent of the prison population in Australia and commit violent crime at 20 times the rate of females. The ability to deal positively with anger and channel aggressive energy in constructive rather than destructive ways are tasks an adolescent male must master if he is to become a mature man.

There are a variety of strategies for dealing with anger. This session explores the responses of aggression, passivity and assertion. Dealing with anger involves understanding aggressive energy, being able to talk about it, and being able to channel it well. This session is not merely about curbing aggressive impulses; it is also about learning to act assertively and express strength creatively rather than violently.

Pastoral Responses

The purpose of this session is to:

- show that anger is an emotion that is neither positive nor negative;
- present an overview of negative and positive ways people deal with anger, including: aggression, passivity and assertiveness;
- encourage the development of positive responses to the feeling of anger.

Supply List

For this session you will need:

- (optional) name tags;
- one copy of Resource 13, "Dealing with Anger Role Plays" (cut on the dashed lines);
- several photos of people expressing anger to supplement the collection brought by the participants;
- copies of Resource 14, "Personal Reflection: Dealing with Anger";

- copies of Resource 15, "Session 3 Small Group Sharing Scenarios";
- three copies of Resource 16, "Friendships with Girls and Women".

Session Outline

Welcome and Meal Sharing (about 45 minutes)

Introduction and Gospel Reading (about 5 minutes)

What Is Anger? (about 35 minutes)

Responses to Anger (about 45 minutes)

Small Group Sharing (about 40 minutes)

Conclusion (about 10 minutes)

Welcome and Meal Sharing

(about 45 minutes)

Casual Meal

Arrange the room with tables for open seating. As the participants arrive, collect the photos of people with angry expressions that they were assigned to bring. Also, pass out name tags if necessary. Encourage the father and son pairs to sit with people who are not in their regular small sharing groups so that they are able to meet and socialise with as many people in the program as possible.

Conduct the meal buffet-style or in any way that works well for your group.

Offer a formal welcome to the participants and say grace before the meal. Then allow the participants to socialise informally until it is time to begin the session.

Session Preparations

During the mealtime, ask for three volunteers to be actors for three scenes of a short role-play to be conducted during this session. Meet with the volunteers separately, assigning roles and explaining scenes from the three parts of Resource 13, "Dealing with Anger Role Plays". Tell them you will be the teacher in each scene. Briefly rehearse the scenes from Resource 13. Tell the volunteers that they will be called on to enact their particular scene later in the session.

Give a 10-minute warning near the end of the mealtime. Ask the participants to clean up their tables and move to the large meeting room for the beginning of the session.

Dealing with Anger 53

Introduction and Gospel Reading

(about 5 minutes)

After everyone is settled, tell them the title of the session, "Dealing with Anger". Say:

When you hear the word *"anger"*, you probably associate it with a negative or even violent experience. But did you ever stop to consider that Jesus himself got angry on occasion? Raise your hand if you can think of a gospel story that tells of Jesus being angry. (Pause.) Let's hear an example many of you probably had in mind.

John 2:13-17

Present the story of Jesus driving out the money-changers from the temple in your own words. Another option is to read the story dramatically while the other facilitator pantomimes Jesus' actions. Say:

The Passover of the Jews was at hand, and Jesus went up to Jerusalem. In the temple, he found those who were selling oxen and sheep and pigeons, and the money-changers at their business. And making a whip of cords, he drove them all, with the sheep and oxen, out of the temple; and he poured out the coins of the money-changers and overturned their tables. And he told those who sold the pigeons, "Take these things away; you shall not make my Father's house a house of trade."

Reflection

Continue:

The story shows that just as any human being might, Jesus felt angry. What caused him to feel this way? Some background here helps: First, we must understand why there were people conducting this type of commerce in the temple. It was a Passover custom at this time for Jews to come to the temple and sacrifice an animal as a sin offering. A rich person would sacrifice a lamb or a cow. For poor people, a small pigeon might be all they could afford. The animals for the Passover offerings were sold in the temple vestibule, often at inflated prices since these were the only animals that were considered unblemished or fit for sacrifice. People who brought animals from their own flocks were often instructed to trade it for a temple animal at a significant loss.

Also, it was against Jewish law to purchase these animals with Roman money, the official government currency. The Jews who came to purchase an animal first had to convert their money from Roman to Jewish currency before they could buy an animal. And the money-changers often charged an exorbitant commission to perform this exchange, thus increasing the temple profits.

Why was Jesus angry? Well, he was certainly aware of the injustice of the business practices involved. In addition, as he pointed to in several other gospel incidents, the people had placed the ritual practice of a law before its heartfelt intention. Was it really worth disrupting God's holy place to conduct such unseemly business?

Jesus did not passively accept the wrong he saw being committed. Rather, he acted with powerful aggression. Do you think his aggressive response was a positive one? When is it okay to respond likewise? Taken to another level, is a physically violent response ever allowed? For example, what if Jesus had physically thrown down the money-changers themselves along with their tables? In this session, we will explore in more detail the feeling of anger and the positive and negative responses that come from it.

Prayer

Ask all to bow their heads in prayer. Say:

Jesus, you felt angry.

You acted aggressively.

We pray that you will show us the proper ways

to handle our anger and channel our aggressions.

We ask this in your name.

Amen.

What Is Anger?

(about 35 minutes)

Photo Display

Arrange the photos the participants have brought in on a long table in the center of the large meeting area. Ask everyone to gather around the table and view the photos or, if the group is large, to walk single file past the table, look briefly at the photos, and return to their seats. Hold up one of the photos you feel best expresses an angry person. Say, for example:

This is the face of anger! Notice the gritting of teeth. Look at the blazing eyes. Imagine this person clenching his fist and sucking air deeply and loudly in and out of his nose. These are some of the characteristics we imagine for a person who is angry.

In fact, **anger is a powerful emotion** (write the boldfaced words on the board). What are some other powerful human emotions or feelings? (Call on volunteers to make suggestions; for example, fear, joy, sadness, and love.) As with any of these emotions, anger causes changes in our bodies. Not only what we can observe on the outside, but inside of us as well. When we feel angry, the adrenal gland located just above the kidneys releases small amounts of chemicals called adrenaline and noradrenaline into our blood stream. These chemicals cause an increase in heart rate and blood pressure. The physical signs of this may be red cheeks, a tight throat, or a quivering voice. What is happening is that our bodies are getting us ready to respond to our feeling angry. There are two basic kinds of responses: we will either run away from the cause of our anger or we will confront it. This is known as flight or fight. (Write: **two basic responses to anger: flight or fight**.)

Dealing with Anger: Stories of Two Fathers and Two Sons

Introduce the father and son pairs who have prepared talks based on Resource 12. Bridge the presentation defining anger and its responses. Say, for example:

Mr. Rogers and his son Jason have prepared a short presentation on times in their lives when they were angry and how they responded to that anger. After their presentation, you will hear other stories about anger from Mr Fredericks and his son Mark.

Ask the first father and son pair to speak for a total of 10 minutes. Then call on the next pair to do the same. Thank each of these volunteers for his participation.

More About Anger

Continue the presentation providing more information on anger. When possible, refer to the presentations of the fathers and sons as you make the following points. Write the boldfaced sentences on the board. Say:

The feeling of anger is neither good nor bad. Anger is a normal emotion that everyone experiences once in a while. The *Catechism of the Catholic Church* states that "passions are natural components of the human psyche; they form the passageway and ensure the connection between the life of the senses and the life of the mind" (#1764). It is *how* you respond to the feeling of anger that may be good or bad. Interestingly, there are both good and bad responses in both the "flight or fight" categories. We will talk about a variety of responses to anger in a few minutes.

Anger is associated with the judgment "Things are not as they should be". We have expectations of how things should be. In the most basic sense, we have expectations that our physical needs will be met: we will be fed, we will have shelter, we will have clothing. We also have expectations for our emotional needs: we will be respected, we will be appreciated, we will have friends, we will be loved. One of the feelings we experience when any of these needs is not met is anger because we believe that "things are not as they should be". We are angry with the person, corporation, government, God, etc., who we think denied us these things.

Anger may provide the energy to do something about those things that are not as they should be. For example, think of the incident involving the St Kilda football player Nicky Winmar. As an Aboriginal man, Winmar was often targeted by the supporters of opposition teams who racially vilified him, just because his skin is a different colour. For years this injustice caused Winmar to *feel* angry. In one match against the Collingwood Football Club this feeling eventually led Winmar to pull up his jumper and point with pride to his black skin. His action led the Australian Football League to introduce rules about racial vilification. His anger led to effective action, and was a major factor in making the AFL more equitable for Aboriginal players.

Males and females experience and respond to anger differently.[8] For example, one study showed that young boys have more and longer-lasting temper tantrums than young girls. Also, little boys generally have more difficulty in calming down after being aroused to anger than girls do. Studies also show that little boys act out aggressively more than girls. What is true for young boys is also true for adult males. Men tend to experience more difficulty dealing with their anger than women. When a man gets angry, it takes about 20 minutes for his heart rate and blood pressure to return to normal. A woman typically calms down in about 10 minutes. Perhaps this difficulty dealing with anger and aggression explains in part why 90 per cent of the convicted felons in prisons are males.

Responses to Anger

(about 45 minutes)

Allow the participants to stand and stretch briefly before continuing. Remind the participants of the two basic responses to anger: flight or fight. Tell them each of these categories contains both positive and negative ways to respond to anger. Then begin a presentation from the following script. Write the boldfaced words on the board.

Script

One response to anger is passivity. **Passivity is a failure to express feelings**. A passive response to the feeling of anger means that you will do nothing about it. This is the "flight" response. Sometimes passivity is an appropriate and healthy choice. For example, if you were in a convenience store and were suddenly confronted by an armed robber, it might make you feel angry along with being scared. Yet, it would no doubt be best to respond passively to the situation lest you get yourself hurt or even killed.

However, in most cases passive response to anger is not healthy. When you do nothing about your anger, the feeling may be driven deep within you and cause long-lasting resentments and possibly health problems. You will likely end up feeling powerless. Your relationship with the person at whom you were angry will undoubtedly be damaged. Can you connect this response with an example you heard tonight?

An opposite response to anger is aggression, a "fight" response. **Aggression is an act of hostility**. It is manifested in several ways; for example, physical aggression may be directed against others (legally defined as assault), against property (vandalism), or against oneself (drug abuse, self-mutilation, suicide attempts). Aggression may also be directed verbally in the forms of threats, name-calling, racial slurs, and the like. These examples usually fall under the category of **uncontrolled aggression**. Uncontrolled aggression occurs when you impulsively express your anger in physically or verbally hostile ways without any concern for the consequences of your actions or the rights and feelings of others. (If possible, try to connect the definition of uncontrolled aggression with an example you heard from one of the father and son talks.)

Controlled aggression is an act of hostility that is made after some reflection or discrimination of choice. Controlled aggression can be either positive or negative. Premeditated murder is a negative example of controlled aggression. Sports like football are also a form of controlled aggression. Since sports teach lessons like camaraderie, fair play and achievement of goals, football is a positive example of controlled aggression when it is played within the rules.

Jesus' example of making a whip out of cords and driving the money-changers and sellers out of the temple was a form of aggression. How would you classify it? As uncontrolled aggression? (Pause.) As controlled aggression? (Pause.) As a negative or positive example of controlled aggression? (Allow one or two volunteers to offer explanations and comments.)

There is response to anger that combines both aggression and passivity. It is known as **passive aggression**. This type of aggression is shown indirectly. It is usually a deceitful response. For example, a child who is angry at a parent may be deliberately uncooperative in a way designed to annoy the parent, but in a way that can't be proven. Passive aggression is also expressed by stubbornness, inefficiency, deliberate forgetfulness, procrastination, and chronic tardiness. This response camouflages a person's hostility. Passive aggression is a way of being aggressive without giving the other person anything tangible to respond to. Because it does nothing to promote resolution of the conflict causing anger, this response is particularly unhealthy, and often quite long-lasting and destructive.

Simulation Exercise

Ask the fathers and sons to stand and face each other. Direct the sons to stand rigidly. Direct each father to put the palm of one hand on his son's chest and push gently. Have the fathers push until they dislodge their sons from their firm grounding. Then have the pairs reverse roles with the sons pushing their fathers.

Call for volunteers among the fathers and sons to summarise their feelings during the exercise as they assumed both roles: the passive resister (being pushed) and the aggressor (doing the pushing).

Continue the presentation from the script.

Script (continued)

A third way to respond to anger is assertion. **Assertion is the act of stating or expressing oneself directly and positively**. In an assertive response to anger, you would respectfully confront the source of your anger; in other words, talk with the person. To talk about your feelings, you tell what has happened and how you feel. You start all of your statements with the word "*I*" (e.g., "I feel angry"), and you try not to use the word "*you*" in an accusing way. You state clearly to the other person what he or she has to do with how you are feeling. An assertive response is simulated when two people look each other in the eye and exchange a firm handshake. (Ask the fathers and sons to face each other and shake hands.) In this experience, you are neither being pushed around, nor aggressively pushing the other around. You are both exercising your power in mutually enhancing ways.

Role Plays

Introduce the three role-plays you prepared during mealtime as a review for ways to respond to anger. Tell the three volunteers that you will enact each scene individually, beginning with scene 1. Hold three pieces of paper as props for detention slips. Then say to the rest of the group:

I would like you to imagine this is a high school classroom. I am the teacher and you are the students. I am trying to teach a lesson, but I am annoyed because some students are disrupting the lesson by talking in class. In each of these scenes, I will target the wrong student for discipline.

Proceed with scene 1. Then ask the group to identify which type of response was enacted (passive aggression). Repeat the process for scene 2 (uncontrolled aggression) and scene 3 (assertion).

Imagination Exercise: Leave Your Anger Behind[9]

Dim the lights in the room. Tell the participants to prepare for an imagination exercise. Ask them to sit straight in their chairs without straining and put their feet flat on the floor. Tell them to shut their eyes and to breathe slowly and deeply. If you have chosen some reflective background music to play, begin playing it now. Read the following imagination story slowly and clearly, pausing between sentences and a bit longer after the questions:

Think of someone who has hurt you and made you feel angry. Recall the incident that angered you, what was done, and what was said. Imagine you see this person sitting right in front of you. Tell him or her of your anger. Express all of your anger as directly as you can. Begin your sentences with the word "I".

Now look at the whole incident from the other person's point of view. Take the other person's place and try to see the incident as he or she would. How does the incident look now? Take some time to really think and feel from the perspective of the other person. What is a new insight you now have about the situation?

Now go to the scene where this incident originally took place. Stay there for a while. Then turn to an image of Jesus on the cross. Look closely at Jesus. Keep alternating between the event that caused you hurt and the scene of Jesus on the cross. Let the resentment slip away. Let a feeling of calm envelop you.

Allow for a few more minutes of silence or music as a conclusion to the exercise.

Personal Reflection

Pass out copies of Resource 14, "Personal Reflection: Dealing with Anger". Read the directions and explain each of the listed exercises. Tell the participants that they will be asked to share and explain what they write or draw with their own father or son. Allow about 10 minutes for individual reflection and writing or drawing.

Father and Son Dialogue

Ask the father and son pairs to move together for "one-to-one" sharing. Tell them to share for about 10 minutes from the Personal Reflection resource using this format:

- One person tells which reflection exercise he chose and then shares what he wrote or drew. The other person asks clarifying questions or offers a personal response to the reflection.
- The process is repeated, with the second person beginning.
- As time allows, the father and son share any other comments, questions, or insights about the material presented to this point in the session.

Small Group Sharing

(about 40 minutes)

Tell the participants that they will be meeting with the same small group that formed at the first session. Give one copy of Resource 15, "Session 3 Small Group Sharing Scenarios", to each participant. Go over the format for the sharing. Say:

You will hear several scenarios that typically cause either fathers or sons to feel angry. The group moderator will read and lead the sharing for each scenario. The group moderator will take suggestions from the group for various passive, aggressive, and assertive responses for each scenario. Then he will ask each person to share how he would respond if confronted with that situation. The process will be repeated for as many scenarios as you have time to cover. There is no need to begin with the first scenario and cover them in order. Choose scenarios that seem important to your group.

Direct the groups to separate areas for the sharing. Tell them they will have about 35 minutes for sharing. After the sharing time, call the participants back to the large meeting area.

Conclusion

(about 10 minutes)

Session Four Preparation

Ask for three fathers to prepare and share short talks about their relationships with women, especially in the areas of friendship and respect. Tell the volunteers to see you at the conclusion of the session for more explanation and to take a copy of Resource 16, "Friendships with Girls and Women".

Concluding Prayer

Ask all to stand and recite together the *Our Father*.

Reminders

Remind the fathers and sons responsible for the casual meal for Session Four to bring the dishes and remind the entire group of the date of the next session. Dismiss them on time.

Session Four

Friendships with Girls & Women

Background Information for Facilitators

Nowadays the word "relationship" is often a code word for sexual relations. When a person speaks of "having a relationship", these words often refer to a sexual encounter. An analysis of adolescent sexuality is not the aim of this session. Rather, this session specifically addresses the area of *friendship* with women, another important aspect of relationship.

From about the age of three years old until puberty, boys and girls tend to form friendships and play with those of the same gender. Puberty not only initiates physical changes, but also alters how boys feel about girls and girls feel about boys. Many adolescent boys worry that their efforts to form friendships with girls will only end in failure, embarrassment, social disgrace or rejection. Many boys have gone years without communicating much with girls. In early adolescence, boys and girls need to be reacquainted with basic relational skills as they seek to establish friendships with one another. Fortunately, the task is not as difficult as one might imagine. Adolescents usually have a great deal of experience in meeting people, making new friends, being friends and maintaining friendships with members of the same sex. These skills transfer well when the time comes for adolescent boys to form friendships with adolescent girls.

This session reviews the qualities and characteristics of true friendship. It offers encouragement for adolescents to review the skills they have already mastered for making same-sex friendships and use them as they form new relationships with the opposite sex. True friends respect one another; that is, they treat each other as they wish to be treated, with the dignity that any person deserves. This session explores these issues through the use of several interpersonal techniques, including a panel discussion focusing on some of the impediments to healthy male-female relationships.

Pastoral Responses

The purpose of this session is to:

- explore the meaning of friendship;
- look at ways that people make friends;
- show how friendship skills apply in relationships between men and women.

Supply List

For this session you will need:

- (optional) name tags;
- a supply of pens or pencils;
- copies of Resource 17, "Personal Reflection: Friendships with Girls and Women" (one for each participant);
- copies of Resource 18, "Session 4 Small Group Sharing Questions";
- copies of Resource 6, "Guidelines for Small Group Sharing";
- three copies of Resource 19, "The Quest for Identity";
- small slips of paper.

Session Outline

Welcome and Meal Sharing (about 45 minutes)

Introduction and Gospel Reading (about 20 minutes)

Making Friends with Girls and Women (about 60 minutes)

Small Group Sharing (about 45 minutes)

Summary and Conclusion (about 10 minutes)

Welcome and Meal Sharing

(about 45 minutes)

Casual Meal

Arrange the room with tables for open seating. As the participants arrive, pass out name tags, if necessary. Encourage the father and son pairs to sit with people they don't know well so that they are able to meet and socialise with as many people in the program as possible.

Conduct the meal buffet-style, or in any way that works well for your group.

Offer a formal welcome to the participants and say grace before the meal. Then allow the participants to socialise informally until it is time to begin the session.

Give a 10-minute warning near the end of the mealtime. Ask the participants to clean up their tables and move to the large meeting room for the beginning of the session.

Introduction and Gospel Reading

(about 20 minutes)

When everyone is settled, introduce the session theme. Say:

The topic for this session is friendship and how we can apply the skills we have used for making and maintaining friendships with other males, to making and maintaining friendships with women. From the time you were very young, you made and formed friendships. This session will help you to recall the skills you used to do these things. Also, we all share a common friend, Jesus. In Jesus, we have a friend who teaches us the ultimate meaning of friendship: he gives his life for us. Let us hear Jesus' words about the challenge of friendship.

John 15:12-15

Read the following words of Jesus slowly and dramatically:

> This is my commandment
>
> that you love one another
>
> as I have loved you.
>
> No one has greater love than this,

to lay down one's life for one's friends.

You are my friends

if you do what I command you.

I do not call you servants any longer,

because the servant does not know

what the master is doing;

but I have called you friends,

because I have made known to you

everything that I have heard from my Father.

Reflection/Imagination Exercise

Continue:

Jesus said that we are no longer servants, but friends. A servant is a person who is submissive to another. You may have had relationships where you treat another that way or were treated that way yourself. On the other hand, the word "friend" has roots in a Germanic word that means "to love". Friendships grow to become caring and loving relationships. This is the relationship we are called to have with God, and in turn with one another.

Let's think of some of the people you have called friends. Please make yourselves comfortable. Sit straight in your chairs without straining and put your feet flat on the floor. Shut your eyes and breathe slowly and deeply as I take you through the following memories (pause between sentences):

Recall the home and neighbourhood you lived in before you went to school. Who were your neighbours? Remember a boy you played with. Was there a girl you played with? What were some of the things you did with these friends? Take a moment to picture your play areas: your homes, your backyards, your neighbourhood.

Now remember kindergarten or Year 1. Can you remember your teacher? Who were your friends in this class? What did you like about these friends? Are you still close to any of them? Think about a time when you played with one of your school friends after school. Were you at home or at your friend's home? What did you do? What did you like about this person?

As you grew, your friendships changed. Think about a conflict you had with a friend as you approached your secondary school years. What caused the conflict? Was the conflict resolved? If so, how? If not, why not? What did this person help you learn about the meaning of friendship?

In your memory, recall the first days of secondary school. This was another occasion for meeting new friends. What led you to begin a friendship with a person you had not met before? What did you like about this person? Think about a lifelong friend who went a different way as you started secondary school. What was the cause of this breakup? Do you think you will ever be close again with this person?

Now think of the person you would call your best or closest friend. (Pause for at least 30 seconds.) Why is this the person who comes to mind? What are some characteristics of this person that you admire? What would it mean for you to lay down your own life for this friend? This doesn't have to mean that you would actually be martyred for your friend. Rather, how do you stand by and support this friend? How does this friend support you?

Thank God for your closest friend. Thank God for all of your friends. Thank God for the gift of friendship.

Prayer

Ask all to bow their heads in prayer. Say:

Jesus,

you called us your friends.

Help us to learn from you the true meaning of friendship

as we continue existing relationships and seek out new ones.

We ask this in your name.

Amen.

Making Friends with Girls and Women

(about 60 minutes)

Continue with a presentation near the board based on the following script.

Script

In the prayer reflection and imagination exercise, you've been thinking about some of the friends in your life. If you're a teenager, it is likely that most of your friends up until now have been boys. As you know, in adolescence your body, mind, and emotions change. You have an attraction to girls that you did not have a few years ago. The attraction takes many forms. You may be attracted to one girl because of the way she looks. You may be drawn to another girl because of her personality, a third because of an interest you share. These attractions are normal and natural and they serve a good purpose: they bring two people together. From that point on, it is up to the two people to get to know one another.

Unfortunately, many guys associate "getting to know" a girl only with sexual behaviour. A term like "scoring" not only has sexual connotations but it implies a relationship based on one person using another for their own pleasure. This type of relationship is actually a form of servitude, as described and disregarded by Jesus in the Gospel passage we have just heard.

Rather, as you begin to be attracted to and meet more girls, remember the goal of coming together with someone you like is friendship. Again, the term "girlfriend" is sometimes a misnomer among teenagers. A girlfriend must not be a person who serves as an object on whom you can act out your sexual feelings. A girlfriend is a friend who is also a girl. Friendship is the basis for all successful relationships between men and women, up to and including marriage.

You may agree with everything that has been said so far, but be holding onto a nagging question: **How can I make friends with the girls I know?** (Write this on the board). No matter how confident a guy seems outwardly, there are always some girls with whom he is too shy or intimidated by to approach and make friends. Fortunately, the skills you have already mastered for making friends from the time you were a young child can help you as you now form friendships with girls.

Large Group Sharing

Ask the participants to think about techniques they have used in the past for meeting new people and making new friends. Call on volunteers to share these ideas with the group. Summarise and write the ideas on the board. Add the following ideas (the boldface words) to the list if they are not mentioned and expand on how each idea for making friends with other boys also works for making friends with girls. Allow input from the fathers as you continue from the script.

Script (continued)

Common Interests You have probably met many of your best mates through your common interests in things like sport, music, surfing, computers and so on. Well, girls like many of the same things that boys do. Join a club or a group of people with whom you have a common interest and that you would enjoy being a part of.

Common Beliefs You can be friends with a person and believe different things and hold different values. But having common beliefs and values does make for a successful friendship. Participating in a church or community service project you believe in can help you to meet people who likely hold some of the same beliefs and values as you.

Focus on the Other Person Part of this skill involves being a good listener. When you listen to someone, don't spend the time thinking about what you will say next. Rather, first comment on what was said. Ask clarifying questions to show the person you are interested. This technique also works with people you don't know as a way to start conversations. You can say to a girl, "I thought you did a great job in the play. How did you get interested in acting?" Or, "You always do well in science. What's your secret?"

Mutual Friends Some boys are able to make friends with girls at an earlier age than others. Ask one of your mates if you can hang out with him when he is with a group of girls. Then just practice the skills of good listening and polite conversation as you get to know the other people in the group.

Relatives If you are shy or uncomfortable around girls, practice talking with some of your female relatives: sisters, cousins, aunts, and even mothers and grandmothers. The communication skills you practice with people you know well will help you as you seek to meet new friends who are girls.

The Golden Rule As with any relationship, if you treat another—boy or girl—the way you wish to be treated, you are likely to have many friends.

Friendships with Girls and Women: Stories of Three Fathers

Introduce the three fathers who have prepared talks based on Resource 16. Build on the theme of making and maintaining friendships between men and women. Say:

Building friendships with women is a worthwhile task that all of you, with practice, are able to accomplish. Now we are going to hear from three fathers who will tell you how they have established friendships with women and how these friendships have enriched their lives.

Ask one father to begin his talk. He will speak for approximately five minutes. Then repeat the procedure with the second and third fathers.

Qualities of Friendship

After the presentations, continue with the group in the large meeting area near the board. Say:

Based on what you heard and on your own experience, what do you feel women want from their friendships with men?

Allow volunteers to offer qualities. Summarise their responses on the board under a heading, **Qualities of Friendship Between a Man and a Woman**. Write as many qualities as you can, including:

- Honesty.
- Forgiveness.
- Love.
- Similar Values.
- Respect.

If not mentioned, add **attraction** to the list. Then, explain. Say:

Initial attraction between a man and a woman is another dimension of friendship. It is an important one, because it is attraction for another on one or both persons' parts that may allow a friendship to get off the ground in the first place. Why are people attracted to some people rather than others? The answers are varied and inconclusive. Some of it has to do with physical attraction: you are attracted by the way another person looks. Other factors attracting one person to another have to do with social behaviour, attitude, personality, similar interests and talents.

Attraction is a necessary and normal part of forming friendships. But strong physical attraction and sexual feelings for another should not in any way infringe on the other qualities of a friendship that we have listed on the board.

Friendships between men and women require mutual respect. Mutual respect means a willingness to show consideration or appreciation. Girls and women will not respect someone who degrades them, abuses them, or is not concerned for their physical, emotional, and spiritual well-being. Mutual respect is an essential quality in all friendships, but especially in a friendship between a man and a woman.

Call on volunteers to comment on how the following words and actions of boys and men can cause disrespect and harm in their relationships with girls and women:

— bragging of sexual exploits, real or imagined

— vocalising social stereotypes about men and women

— viewing pornography

Personal Reflection

Pass out copies of Resource 17, "Personal Reflection: Friendships with Girls and Women". Read the directions and explain each of the listed exercises. Tell the participants that they will be asked to share and explain what they write with their own father or son. Allow about 10 minutes for individual reflection and writing.

Father and Son Dialogue

Ask the father and son pairs to move together for "one-to-one" sharing. Tell them to share for about 10 minutes from the Personal Reflection resource using this format:

- One person tells which reflection exercise he chose and then shares what he wrote or drew. The other person asks clarifying questions or offers a personal response to the reflection.

- The process is repeated, with the second person beginning.

- As time allows, the father and son share any other comments, questions, or insights about the material presented to this point in the session.

Small Group Sharing

(about 45 minutes)

Distribute copies of Resource 6, "Guidelines for Small Group Sharing" and review each of the guidelines. Pass out a copy of Resource 18, "Session 4 Small Group Sharing Questions", to each participant. Read the directions. Direct the participants to areas for small group sharing with their assigned groups. Tell them they will have about 45 minutes for sharing.

Summary and Conclusion

(about 10 minutes)

Ask the participants to meet in the large meeting area near the board. Pass out two slips of paper to each person. Ask them to finish each of the following sentences (write on the board). Tell them they don't have to sign the slips but can if they want to. Use these completed sentences to help you evaluate the session.

Something new I learned at this session was . . .

This session could be improved by . . .

Session Five Preparation

Say to the fathers:

For Session Five, you will need to describe what your son was like as an infant. Also, plan to speak briefly on how you felt on the day of his birth. To accompany this short talk, please bring at least one photo of your son when he was young.

Also, ask three or four fathers to volunteer to bring to Session Five short video clips of their sons during infancy. Tell them to cue a one to two-minute video segment that will be viewed by all the participants at the next session.

Privately ask three sons to prepare talks for Session Five on their quest for personal identity. Choose teens with a high level of maturity and some natural ability to speak before a group. Provide each teen with a copy of Resource 19, "The Quest for Identity", to help them prepare.

Concluding Prayer

Lead the following prayer:

> God, you have called us to be friends
> with you and one another.
> Please help us to grow in friendship
> with the females in our lives as we
> treat them with love and respect.
> We ask this in the name of Jesus, your Son,
> and our brother.
> Amen.

Reminders

Remind the fathers and sons responsible for casual meal dishes for Session Five to bring them. Be sure all the participants know the date of the next session.

Session Five

The Quest for Identity

Background Information for Facilitators

The psychosocial task of adolescence and early adulthood is identity achievement—finding out who one is. For the male, adolescence is a period of great change, both physically and psychologically, as he relinquishes his identity as a boy and begins to take on his new identity as a man.

His identity, or his sense of self, is achieved through a self-reflective process by which the adolescent attempts to learn about himself through an understanding of his personal history, his place in the world and his possibilities for the future. This process of self-reflection is also a spiritual one. In the words of St. Anthony of Egypt: "For all who know themselves know that they are of one immortal substance."

The process of identity achievement for an adolescent male usually takes up the whole of his teenage years, and often extends into early adulthood. It involves:

- deciding on and preparing for a future occupation;
- taking responsibility for himself and his actions;
- seeing himself in a socially acceptable role that embodies his own values and those of his community;
- being faithful to his commitments.

Identity achievement is a relational process as well as a subjective one. The adult generation has an important role to play in the identity struggles of adolescent children. Research shows that parents who clearly signal their ideals and values to their adolescent children, and who relate well to them, help them very much in the task of achieving personal identity.

One of the ways a father can assist his adolescent son achieve a secure sense of identity is to tell him the story of his birth and early infancy. For the vast majority of teenagers hearing this story, and hearing about how their parents felt about them, it can give them a repository of basic hopefulness that will sustain them as they make their way into adulthood. The story of the son's unremembered self suggests a new future self he could shape for himself. In this session, the fathers share these stories with their sons. (*Note:* Special provisions are needed for teens attending the program with mentors. The mentor will need to meet the boy's mother to learn the story of his birth and infancy, so that it can be shared during the session.)

Another aspect of identity achievement is the ongoing process of recognising and claiming one's deepest aspirations. One of the important things a person does during adolescence is daydream about who he could be. In this way, he "tries on different hats" in his imagination and begins to work out that to which he aspires. For instance, he might imagine himself as an actor, or a professional athlete, or a businessman, or a priest, or a father and so on. These aspirations are one way in which he begins to define himself. As he sifts his aspirations, discarding some and settling on others, they begin to shape his life and direct his actions, drawing him on. It is critical that the adolescent male not live out his father's ambitions for him, or anyone else's either. This session is designed to help each of the sons reflect on his life story and look at where he wants his life to lead.

Pastoral Responses

The purpose of this session is to:

- allow fathers the chance to share the stories of their sons' birth;
- help fathers and sons recognise and claim their deepest life ambitions.

Supply List

For this session you will need:

- (optional) name tags;
- small slips of paper with each father's name written on one;
- a hat;
- copies of Resource 20, "Session 5 Small Group Sharing of Memories" cut on the dashed line;
- a supply of pens or pencils;
- scissors;
- (optional) a recording of reflective music to accompany an imagination exercise;
- (optional) CD player;
- copies of Resource 21, "Personal Reflection: My Life History".

Session Outline

Welcome and Meal Sharing (about 45 minutes)

Introduction and Gospel Reflection (about 10 minutes)

Remembering Me (about 25 minutes)

Small Group Sharing (about 45 minutes)

Becoming Me (about 50 minutes)

Conclusion (about 5 minutes)

Welcome and Meal Sharing

(about 45 minutes)

Casual Meal

Arrange the room with tables for open seating. As the participants arrive, pass out name tags, if necessary. Encourage the father and son pairs to sit with a new mix of people so that they are able to meet and socialise with as many people in the program as possible.

Conduct the meal buffet-style, or in any way that works well for your group.

Offer a formal welcome to the participants and say grace before the meal. Then allow the participants to socialise informally until it is time to begin the session.

Video Preparation

Speak with the fathers who have brought one to two-minute video clips of their sons in infancy. Make sure that each video is cued to the starting place. Ask each father to prepare a brief statement to introduce the clip of his son.

Give a 10-minute warning near the end of the mealtime. Ask the participants to clean off their tables and move to the large meeting room for the beginning of the session.

Introduction and Gospel Reflection

(about 10 minutes)

When everyone is seated, introduce the main theme of the session. Say:

This session is called "The Quest for Identity". Let's think for a moment about what we mean by the words **quest** and **identity**. In medieval times, a quest was an expedition undertaken by a knight in order to search out and perform a great feat. For us, quest means seeking and pursuing an understanding of who God calls us to be, our identity. Identity refers to our sense of who we are. We learn about our identity through an exploration of our past, our current experiences, and our dreams for the future. We achieve the fruits of our quest for identity when we are able to confidently answer the question: "Who am I?"

Jesus, himself, asked this question in an attempt to understand his own identity as both a man born of human parents and the divine Son of his Father in heaven. Let's hear the scripture passage that tells of Jesus' questioning of his disciples.

Mark 8:27-33

Present the following exchange between Jesus and Peter in your own words or read them dramatically. Or, take the part of Jesus while the other facilitator takes the part of the disciples and Peter.

Jesus went on with his disciples to the villages of Caesarea Philippi; and on the way he asked his disciples, "Who do people say that I am?" And they answered him, "John the Baptist; and others, Elijah; and still others, one of the prophets." He asked them, "But who do you say that I am?" Peter answered him, "You are the Messiah." And he sternly ordered them not to tell anyone about him.

Then he began to teach them that the Son of Man must undergo great suffering, and be rejected by the elders, the chief priests, and the scribes, and be killed, and after three days rise again. He said all this quite openly. And Peter took him aside and began to rebuke him. But turning and looking at his disciples, he rebuked Peter and said, "Get behind me, Satan! For you are setting your mind not on divine things but on human things."

Reflection

Continue:

Like anyone, Jesus wondered about his identity. Through prayer and introspection, he certainly must have had many ideas about who he was. Still, he wanted to hear the opinions of others. First, he asked his disciples who the crowds thought he was. He listened to the answers but soon dismissed them, asking a second question. "Who do you say that I am?" he asked his closest friend. Peter's answer struck a chord with Jesus' personal reflections about his own identity. When Peter answers, "You are the Christ", one has the sense that Jesus needed his feedback to know who he was. He was trying to learn who he was from the significant people in his life.

As each of you continues his own quest for identity and tries to answer the question "Who am I?", it is important to remember Jesus' example: He sought out the opinion of others. This is a model for you to use as well. Adolescents especially, can use the help of their fathers as they try to answer this vital question for themselves.

However, notice the conclusion of this passage. Though Peter correctly named Jesus as the Christ or Messiah foretold by the prophets of old, he did not really grasp all that being the Christ would entail for Jesus. Peter likely envisioned the Christ and his followers establishing a lifestyle of riches and worldly power. Jesus said it would be just the opposite: he would be rejected, put to death, and later rise from the dead. When Peter can't accept these difficult words, Jesus reprimands him in as strong a language as possible.

Think of this part of the scenario in relation to your own quest. You, too, will hear from many people who will help you to define who you are. Your peers, for example, can help. They can encourage you to explore all of your talents and to try new things. But peers can also have a false understanding of who you are. They may encourage you to try things that do not help you know the real you; drug use will only mask your real feelings and may wipe out real talents; inappropriate sexual behaviour will keep you from achieving real, emotionally intimate relationships with women; materialism will lead you to believe that what you own is more important than who you are. Even a father who has a very good idea of who his son is will not know everything about him.

In terms of the question "Who am I?", it is very important for each person to come to his own final, personal answer. Your identity is your own. As God created you as the one and only you, so too your identity is yours and yours alone.

Remembering Me

(about 25 minutes)

Continue in the large meeting area near the television. Say:

Part of answering the question "Who am I?" involves viewing our lives in their totality, from beginning to end, the past to the present to the future. Unfortunately, this means we have a big hole in our story because we cannot remember our infancy and early childhood. Fortunately, we have photographs, videos, and most importantly, the memories of those who were present with us in those years—our parents and relatives—to help us learn what we were like.

Video Presentation

Cue the first video with a one to two-minute clip of one of the sons when he was an infant. Ask the father to briefly introduce the context of the scene that will be shown. Then play the video clip. Repeat with introductions and playing of the other video clips.

Sentence Starters

Write the following sentence starters on the board:

In the year my son was born,

the political climate was . . .

the big sports story was . . .

a popular movie was . . .

one type of music teenagers enjoyed was . . .

a world tragedy that occurred was . . .

a popular television program was . . .

society was different because . . .

Say:

To get a broader perspective of what things were like when the sons in this room were born, let's hear how some fathers answer the following questions. Fathers, I have your names in a hat. If I pick your name, please finish one of these sentences to help us have a clearer understanding of what times were like when your son was born.

Pick a name from the hat and ask that father to respond to any of the questions. You may wish to put a check mark by each sentence as it is finished and encourage the other respondents to finish the other sentences. Continue with the process for about 15 minutes or until you have a good idea of what things were like when the sons were infants.

Small Group Sharing

(about 45 minutes)

Tell the participants they will be meeting with their regular small groups for personal sharing of memories about their sons' births and infancy. Tell the fathers to bring the photo(s) of their sons to the small group meeting place. Pass out copies of both halves of Resource 20, "Session 5 Small Group Sharing of Memories", to the group moderators. Ask the representatives to distribute the appropriate parts of the resource to the fathers and sons. Read the directions. Explain the format for sharing. Say:

Go around the group sharing *one* memory as alluded to on the resource. If there is time, go around a second time and a third time, telling about other memories.

Give a five-minute warning prior to the end of the time reserved for small group sharing.

Becoming Me

(about 50 minutes)

Ask the participants to meet in the large meeting area near the board. Say:

In the opening part of the session and in your small group sharing, you looked to your past to help you answer the question "Who am I?" Of course, this is only part of the process necessary to fill in your life story. Currently the adolescents in this room are in a key time of life for identity achievement. This is an "in-between" stage in life when males are neither boys nor men, but rather are able to look back at who they have been and look forward imagining and working to become the men they want to be.

Please listen to a story about the transition from boyhood to manhood.

Tell the following story in your own words.

Son of the Tribe Story[10]

The African youth listened eagerly to the instructions. It was the most important moment in his life—the rite that was to make him a man. He had reached puberty, and now to be accepted into the tribe as a full-fledged adult member, he had to pass the traditional test that would show he was strong, sensible, responsible, and trustworthy. If he failed the test he would continue to be a child for another season, in the shame of his failure and the impatience of the long wait. That is why he was listening with rapt attention, ready to carry out with prompt exactness the secret orders given by the elders of the tribe.

These were the instructions: he had to walk alone into the jungle, without bow and arrows, without spear and shield, and wander and roam through it till he saw, and was seen by, a lion, a rhinoceros, a python, and an elephant. In no case would he defend himself or run away, and he would take no food, however alluring the fruits of the trees he saw. Once he had achieved the four goals, he had to come back immediately and report to the tribe. That was all.

The young man departed at once, and directed his steps toward the high-grass prairies where he knew lions waited for their prey, and where it would not be difficult for him to see the king of the jungle and be seen by him. Soon he saw a lion lounging under a tree in the carefree majesty of his lofty presence. He held his breath and waited till the lion would deign to look at him. At last the lion lifted his head, swept the horizon with his gaze, and fixed it for an instant on the svelte erect figure of the motionless youth. Their eyes met, the candidate for manhood and the king of the jungle were eye-to-eye, face-to-face in mutual recognition. The young man made sure that the lion had looked at him in order to be able to attest it before the tribe, and moved back slowly into the jungle, knowing that he had already achieved the most difficult part of his mission.

Deep in the jungle he saw a large python wound around a tree, and held its gaze without blinking. He also knew the haunts of the rhinoceros, and watched him, and knew that he himself was watched in the tense air of mistrust and warning that surrounds this dangerous creature. Now only the easiest part of the job remained, the elephant. There were many around the place, and it would not be long before he would meet a herd or a lonely male, and make himself prudently seen. He knew that the elephant does not attack unless attacked first. It was enough to find one and the task would be over. But he could not find any. He went through all the likely places, searched for footprints, scanned the horizon, waited at water holes, but he did not succeed in sighting a single elephant.

For the first time he began to feel hungry. Till that moment he had not counted days or nights, had not felt hunger, but as the search prolonged itself and fear of failure began to rise in him, he began to feel weak. How long could he keep up this search? What would he do if he did not find an elephant? He would prefer to die of hunger in the solitude of the jungle, and so save his dignity if he could not save his life; but the orders he had received commanded him to return alive to the village and report truthfully on all that had happened.

He held on to the very last moment, but he did not succeed in sighting an elephant, and he came back sad and crestfallen to tell the tribe his misery. After listening to him, the chief spoke: "You have passed the test. We knew that you would not meet an elephant because we had beforehand scared them all away from the whole region. The test was not seeing the animals, but telling the truth, and you have said it. From this moment on, you are one of us in full dignity and right. You are a son of the tribe."

After the story, continue with a presentation from the following script. Write the boldface words on the board under the heading **Becoming Me**.

Script

The story points out several factors that are involved in the process of achieving identity.

First, achieving identity means **being truthful**. Not only was the boy in the story truthful with his elders, but more importantly, he was truthful with himself. Have you ever heard the expression "believing your own lie"? This means that some people lie even to themselves about their own dreams, talents, and skills. Being truthful means making an honest assessment of your dreams, talents and skills and looking for ways they can be applied in the future in your relationship with others, in a career and in Christian living.

Achieving identity also involves **testing**. Like the boy in the story, adolescents today will also "try themselves out" as men. Most will experience a need to explore all the possibilities of their personality and to test their personal limits.

Unfortunately, some adolescents test themselves in dangerous ways, being dared into foolish activities by their peer group. Many adolescents risk themselves by experimenting with drugs, participating in inappropriate sexual relations, driving a car too fast, drinking too much alcohol and many other life-threatening behaviours. On the other hand, testing can be a positive and worthwhile experience. Working at an after-school job, engaging in sports or other physical activities such as skate-boarding, surfing or abseiling, learning computer or mechanical skills, and pursuing intellectual interests are positive ways adolescents try themselves out as men.

Assertion is another aspect of achieving identity. Remember, assertion is "the thoughtful expression of one's legitimate desires and feelings that enhance both you and another". Identity achievement is a form of assertion. For adolescents, it means expressing legitimate desires and feelings about who *you* would like to be in a way that enhances you and others.

Practically, this means asserting your right to tell your own story, and to decide who you wish to be in the future.

Quest for Identity: Stories of Three Sons

Introduce the teens who have prepared talks based on Resource 19. Draw on the points listed on the board. Say, for example:

One way to describe the process of "becoming me" is to say we are "fulfilling our dreams". Joe Riley will tell about some of his own personal dreams for himself and the future.

Call the first speaker before the group. After five minutes, thank him for his presentation and call the next speaker. Repeat the same format.

Imagination Exercise

Tell the participants to prepare for an imagination exercise (sit up straight, put their feet flat on the floor, shut their eyes, breathe slowly and deeply, etc.) Begin playing a recording of reflective music. Read the following text slowly and clearly, pausing significantly between sentences. Say:

In the following imagination exercise, we are going to explore our aspirations or dreams for the future.

Imagine a holy and peaceful place. It could be an imaginary place or an actual sacred place you have visited, such as a church or somewhere beautiful in nature. In this place, you feel God's presence. Feel yourself kneeling before God. Hear yourself telling God all the great plans you have for your life. What you hope to accomplish in school. What you hope to accomplish in a career. What you hope to accomplish in your relationships with friends. What you hope for in your vocation as a married person (or a single person, or a priest, or a religious brother). What you hope for in your relationship with God. Go back over some of these areas and imagine yourself accomplishing great things. Imagine yourself meeting all of your expectations and more.

Continue playing the reflective music for three to five minutes, or until you detect some restlessness.

Personal Reflection

Pass out copies of Resource 21, "Personal Reflection: My Life History". Go over the directions. Remind the participants that they can use words or symbols to designate high and low events in their lives. Tell the participants they will be sharing this reflection one-on-one with their father or son. Allow about 10 minutes for individual marking of the chart.

Father and Son Dialogue

Ask the father and son pairs to move together for "one-to-one" sharing. Tell them to share for about 10 minutes from the Personal Reflection resource using the following format:

- Place the resources on the floor or table in front of you so that you can each read both charts.

- One person begins, pointing to a word or symbol on the other person's sheet and asking him to explain its meaning.

- Keep taking turns using the same format until time is called.

Conclusion

(about 5 minutes)

Session Six Preparation

Inform the participants that Session Six does *not* begin with a casual meal. Rather, it concludes with a party after a blessing ritual. Adapt the nature of the party to your own needs. For example, if you wish to purchase pizzas and soft drinks, you may want to collect money from the participants at this time. See the "Social Event" section of Session Six, page 89, for more information.

Concluding Prayer

Ask the participants to stand and bow their heads. Lead the following prayer:

Jesus, bless us as we continue our quest for identity.

Help us to be men of faith who always seek the truth

and ever reach for our dreams.

We ask this in your name.

Amen.

Session Six

The Blessing
Ritual

Background Information for Facilitators

Everyone needs affirmation. We have a need to be recognised for our unique talents and gifts. Also, we have a need to be affirmed at times when our gifts and talents are not so visible. This is especially important for teenagers whose skin may be blemished with acne, whose dress and haircut are a cross between what is tolerated by parents and what is admired by peers, whose transition to secondary school has been difficult. Adolescent males, in particular, need to be noticed, affirmed, delighted in, and admired by their fathers and other suitable male role models from the family and the Christian community. Sons need to relate with their fathers on an intimate level, and to receive from them a sense of personal recognition as men-in-the-making. This is one meaning of *blessing*, to praise and desire good fortune for another person.

This final meeting between fathers and sons allows for mutual affirmation and a blessing of sons by fathers using several familiar liturgical rites. These rites can stand on their own or be used within a celebration of Eucharist. If you do choose to have a Eucharist, allow the priest the opportunity to sufficiently preview the material on these pages to familiarise himself with the major themes and rites of this liturgy. In addition, this final gathering of the participants provides them with the opportunity to offer an evaluation of the program and suggestions for future programs of this kind. After the blessing ritual, it is recommended that a party or opportunity for informal socialising be held so as to offer an upbeat end to the program. Several suggestions are offered in the section labeled "Social Event".

Grandfathers. If some of the grandfathers can be present at the Blessing Ritual, then having the three generations participate can be a powerful symbol of fathering happening down the generations. The facilitators adjust the Blessing Ritual to include grandfathers.

Pastoral Responses

The purpose of this session is to:

- evaluate the program;
- allow fathers and sons to reconcile any lingering hurts between one another;
- offer fathers the opportunity to bless their sons through foot washing and laying on of hands;
- socialise in an informal setting.

Supply List

For this session you will need:

- (optional) name tags;
- a supply of pens or pencils;
- copies of Resource 22, "Program Evaluation" (one for each participant);
- (optional) index cards;
- (optional) a fireproof urn;
- (optional) matches;
- pitchers filled with warm water (one for every four fathers);

- basins for foot washing (one for every four fathers);
- towels (one for each father);
- chairs for the sons to sit on during the washing of feet (arranged in groups of four) in the place reserved for the Blessing Ritual;
- copies of Resource 23, "Prayer of Affirmation" (one for every two participants, cut on the dashed line);
- letter quality paper;
- envelopes;
- recording of reflective liturgical music (e.g., Gregorian chant, Taizé);
- tape or CD player.

Session Outline

Welcome and Evaluation of the Program (about 20 minutes)

Blessing Ritual (about 90 minutes if Mass is included, less if not)

Social Event (times will vary)

Welcome and Evaluation of the Program

(about 20 minutes)

Begin the session in the large meeting room. Greet the participants as they arrive. Tell them that they are going to spend the first minutes of the session briefly evaluating the program. Write key words to express the expectations named for the program in Session One (see page 31). Comment briefly from your own perspective on how these expectations were met.

Program Evaluation

Pass out a copy of Resource 22 to each participant. Read the directions. Allow about 10 minutes for the participants to work on their own to write evaluations. When completed, collect the evaluations and use them as helps in planning and conducting future *Between Fathers and Sons* programs.

Note: Experience has shown that it is better to do the evaluations before the blessing rituals and social event so that this rather perfunctory task does not interfere with the celebratory atmosphere of this session. It is recommended that you attempt to get some feedback on the blessing rituals from the participants at the social function in order to be able to evaluate and improve upon it in the future.

Introduction

Next, briefly explain the word blessing as a "call of God's favour". Say:

We are going to prayerfully affirm the favour that God has for each one of us. To do so, we will be participating in several very familiar and some less familiar prayer rituals, all practiced faithfully by the church over the centuries. These blessings affirm that God created you in his likeness, and that you are loved.

Direct the participants to the area you have reserved for the Blessing Ritual. (If possible, conduct the Blessing Ritual in the church sanctuary or a chapel.)

Blessing Ritual

(about 90 minutes)

Play the recording of reflective music as the participants enter the space for prayer. Gregorian chant has a calming effect and tends to quiet the group. If the blessing ritual will take place in the context of a Eucharist, the priest can serve as leader, or may call upon the facilitators to do so. If the blessing ritual will stand alone, the facilitators alternate in the role of leader. The parts that are specifically for the Presider in a Eucharistic celebration are scripted as leader.

Opening

Leader: We come together

in the name of the Father,

and of the Son,

and of the Holy Spirit.

All: Amen.

Leader: May the peace of Jesus Christ be with you.

All: And also with you.

Examination of Father and Son Relationships

Ask everyone to be seated. Lead an examination of father and son relationships. Say:

Think about a word or phrase that describes the hurtful times in your relationship with your father or son based on the following statements. (Pause between each of the following statements.)

Statements

- a hurt caused by a promise not kept
- a hurt caused when you were too busy to spend time together
- a hurt caused by lack of cooperation
- a hurt caused by a family argument or break-up
- a hurt caused by one person placing unrealistic demands on the other
- a hurt caused by harsh words
- a hurt caused by violence
- a hurt caused by a lack of communication

Optional: Have the participants write words or short phrases on index cards to represent the hurts described above. Prior to the rite of reconciliation, have them place the cards in a metal urn. Set the cards on fire, symbolising a removal of these hurts from their lives.

Rite of Reconciliation

Ask the father and son pairs to stand and face each other, at least six feet apart from other pairs so that they can speak privately. Then, say:

You have thought about the hurts that have come between you. Looking at each other, man to man, take turns expressing your sorrow. Begin one or more statements with "I am sorry". Express some of the hurts you named.

Allow about five minutes. Then, ask the fathers and sons to place their right hands on each other's shoulders as you conduct any form of penitential rite, for example:

Leader: For the times we have failed to listen to each other and failed to understand.

    Lord, have mercy.

  All: Lord, have mercy.

Leader: For the times we have failed to keep our promises to each other.

    Christ, have mercy.

  All: Christ, have mercy.

Leader: For the times we have failed to appreciate and respect each other.

    Lord, have mercy.

  All: Lord, have mercy.

Leader: Let us pray.

    God our Father,

    source of all life and all love,

    in the lives of these fathers and sons you have given us a glimpse

    of the wonder of your creation.

    Let them always be a reminder to us of your power and love.

    We make this prayer through Christ, our Lord.

  All: Amen.

Gospel Reading

Ask the participants to remain standing for the Gospel reading from John 13:4-15.

Leader: The Lord be with you.

  All: And also with you.

Leader: A reading from the holy gospel according to John.

  All: Glory to you, Lord.

Leader: Jesus, knowing that the Father had given all things into his hands, and that he had come from God and was going to God, got up from the table, took off his outer robe, and tied a towel around himself. Then he poured water into a basin and began to wash the disciples' feet and to wipe them with the towel that was tied around him.

He came to Simon Peter, who said to him, "Lord, are you going to wash my feet?" Jesus answered, "You do not know now what I am doing, but later you will understand." Peter said to him, "You will never wash my feet." Jesus answered, "Unless I wash you, you have no share with me." Simon Peter said to him, "Lord, not my feet only but also my hands and my head!" Jesus said to him, "One who has bathed does not need to wash, except for the feet, but is entirely clean. And you are clean, though not all of you." For he knew who was to betray him; for this reason he said, "Not all of you are clean."

After he had washed their feet, had put on his robe, and had returned to the table, he said to them, "Do you know what I have done to you? You call me Teacher and Lord—and you are right, for that is what I am. So if I, your Lord and Teacher, have washed your feet, you also ought to wash one another's feet. For I have set you an example, that you also should do as I have done to you."

The Gospel of the Lord.

All: Praise to you, Lord Jesus Christ.

The leader offers a brief reflection based on the following script. The participants are seated.

Homily Script

Have you ever had to wash your own feet after walking bare-footed on a summer's day? The filth builds up: dirt from the road layers your heels and soles, small stones bury themselves into the crevices of your toes.

Now imagine washing the feet of another given those conditions and even worse. In Jesus' time, the feet were regarded as a defiled part of the human body. It was thought that a person could "catch" the disease of leprosy just by walking the same ground as lepers. A person visiting the home of another would wash his own feet carefully before entering the house. However, for anyone other than a slave, offering to wash the feet of another was practically unheard of.

Jesus' example tells us several things. First, it shows Jesus taking the role of a servant. Also, by washing the feet of his friends, Jesus was saying: "I love you. I respect you. There is nothing about you I consider unworthy. I accept you as you are."

Fathers, think about what Jesus' example means for you in your relationship with your son. Think how you can say to him (pause between each sentence): "I love you. I respect you. There is nothing about you I consider unworthy. I accept you for who you are."

Fathers, to symbolically show your son that you love, respect, and accept him, I am going to ask you to wash the feet of your son. Son, by allowing your father to wash your feet, you will be acknowledging that you want and need his acceptance, respect, and love.

Foot Washing Ceremony

A pitcher of water, a basin, and four towels are placed at each station of chairs. The sons take a seat in any chair and remove their shoes and socks. When all are seated, say:

The fathers of the sons seated at the far left in each group will come first and pour water over their sons' feet into the basin, and dry their feet with the towel. Sons, when your feet have been washed, you can put your socks and shoes back on. As the first father in each group finishes, the next father should come forward to wash his son's feet. Continue in that way until all the sons have had their feet washed by their fathers.

Play a recording of reflective music during the feet washing ceremony. If a grandfather is present maybe he first will wash the feet of his son, who will in turn wash his son's feet.

Prayer of Affirmation/Prayer of the Faithful

Ask everyone to have a seat. Explain that the next part of the blessing ritual will be the Prayers of the Faithful, a time when everyone gathered will have the opportunity to pray for their personal needs and the needs of others. Distribute letter quality paper, envelopes, pens, and the appropriate halves of Resource 23, "Prayer of Affirmation", to the fathers and sons. Say:

As part of our prayers of the faithful, I would like the fathers to write a prayer for their sons and the sons to write a prayer for their fathers. These prayers should be personal affirmations of your mutual love and respect for one another. You can use the examples on the resource sheet for ideas or you can use any other style you wish. You will not share the specific contents of the letter with the group. The letters will later be read privately.

Allow the participants to move to nearby places where they can be alone for about 10 to 15 minutes of writing. When finished, tell the participants to put their letters in the envelopes and address and seal them. Ask them to write the recipient's name on the envelope. Collect and save all of the sealed envelopes. Ask everyone to stand. Continue as follows:

> Leader: Let us pray
>> for the strength
>> to always be true to our inner selves.
>> Lord hear us.
>
> All: Lord, hear our prayer.
>
> Leader: Let us pray
>> for help for fathers
>> as they guide and help their sons
>> to become mature men.
>> Lord hear us.
>
> All: Lord, hear our prayer.
>
> Leader: Let us pray
>> for these sons

> as they become strong and upright men of God.
>
> Lord hear us.
>
> All: Lord, hear our prayer.

Leader: What else shall we pray for? Please feel free to mention personal intentions for yourself, your father or your son.

Continue in the same format, responding to each prayer "Lord, hear our prayer."

Leader: God, thank you for hearing us.

> Help us to always understand the length and the breadth,
>
> the height and the depth of Jesus' love for us.
>
> We ask this in his name.
>
> All: Amen.

Eucharist

If the Prayer Celebration is part of Eucharist, continue with the liturgy of the Eucharist at this point. If not, move directly to the *Our Father*.

Our Father

Ask the participants to join hands and say together the Lord's Prayer.

Prayer for Peace

Leader: Lord Jesus Christ, who said to your Apostles, Peace I leave you, my peace I give you, look not on our sins, but on the faith of your Church, and graciously grant her peace and unity in accordance with your will. Who live and reign for ever and ever.

All: Amen.

Leader: Let us offer one another a sign of Christ's peace.

Allow a brief time for an exchange of a peace (handshakes, hugs, etc.).

Reading of the Letters of Affirmation

Ask everyone to be seated. Play some soft music. Divide the affirmation letters among the facilitators and distribute them to the participants. (The reading of the letters takes place after communion if the Blessing Ritual is part of Eucharist.)

You can read your letter as the music plays. Remember to keep them. They will likely mean even more to you in the future.

Final Prayer and Blessing

Ask the father and son pairs to stand facing each other for the final prayer:

Leader: Sons, bow your heads and pray silently, thanking God for the gift of manhood. Fathers, place both of your hands on your son's head and pray silently, thanking God for the gift of your son.

Allow a brief time for silent prayer. If a grandfather is participating, ask him to stand behind his son and lay his hands on his son's shoulders as his son lays his hands on his grandson's head. Then, ask the participants to face the front for the final blessing:

Leader: May the Lord be in our hearts and on our lips,

    so that wherever we go

    and whatever we do,

    in the midst of the most ordinary human affairs,

    we may all be known as men who belong to Christ.

  All: Amen.

Leader: May the blessing of Almighty God,

    Father, Son, and Holy Spirit,

    come down on us

    and remain with us forever.

  All: Amen.

Leader: Let us go in peace

    to grow in the love and service of Christ our Lord.

  All: Amen.

Social Event

Offer words of thanks and farewells to the participants before the social event. Give some careful thought and planning to the event so that it will allow for informal sharing among all the participants. You may wish to hold the event at another setting; for example, at the home of one of the participants. Make sure to make all necessary arrangements prior to this final meeting. Listed below are some general suggestions:

        Pool party   Pizzas

        Barbecue   Football

        Backyard cricket

Appendix

Weekend Retreat

The *Between Fathers and Sons* program can be conducted as a weekend retreat. Follow the normal preparations necessary for an overnight retreat (e.g., retreat site, food, transportation, etc.). It is preferable to find a location with rooms with two beds, so that fathers can share rooms with their sons. Other preparations include:

Materials

Collect and assemble all the materials suggested for Sessions One to Five and the Blessing Ritual.

Briefing Meeting for Fathers and Sons

Conduct the Briefing Meeting at least one week prior to the weekend retreat. Arrange for fathers and sons to give presentations as called for in the various sessions. Provide these volunteers with the appropriate resources from the Photocopy section. Also, remind all the fathers to photo a bring or video of their sons as infants and to prepare a short remembrance of his birth or his first years.

Prohibited Items

At the Briefing Meeting, list items that are prohibited on the weekend retreat, including: laptops, PlayStations, homework, books or magazines, and alcohol or other drugs.

Sample Schedule

FRIDAY EVENING

7.00 pm	Arrival; allocation of rooms; name tags given out.
7:30 pm	Session 1: The Father and Son Bond
10:30 pm	Lights out

SATURDAY

8.00 am	Breakfast
9.00 am	Session 2: Becoming a Man
12:30 pm	Lunch and long break
3.00 pm	Session 3: Dealing with Aggression
6.00 pm	Dinner
7:30 pm	Session 4: Friendships with Girls and Women
9:30 pm	Party
10:30 pm	Bed

SUNDAY

8.00 am	Breakfast

9.00 am	Session 5: The Quest for Identity
12:30 pm	Lunch
1:30 pm	Session 6: The Blessing Ritual
3.00 pm	Cleaning and packing up
4.00 pm	Departure

Three One-Day Workshops

The *Between Fathers and Sons* program can operate as three one-day workshops. This plan works well for three consecutive Saturdays, for example. The settings needed for the workshops are the same as suggested for the six-week program. Other preparations include:

Materials

Collect and assemble all the materials suggested for Sessions One to Five and the Blessing Ritual.

Briefing Meeting for Fathers and Sons

Conduct the Briefing Meeting at least one week prior to the first workshop. Arrange for fathers and sons to give presentations as called for in the various sessions. Provide these volunteers with the appropriate resources from the Photocopy section and tell them on which day they will be making their presentations. Also, remind all the fathers to bring a photo or video of their sons as infants and to prepare a short remembrance of his birth or his first years for Session Five (day three).

Casual Meal

Assign the various components of a casual meal (main course, salad, dessert, etc.) to cover each of the three days of the workshop.

Sample Schedule

DAY ONE

9.00 am	Session 1: The Father and Son Bond
12:30 pm	Lunch
1:30 pm	Session 2: Becoming A Man
4:30 pm	Closure

DAY TWO

9.00 am	Session 3: Dealing with Aggression
12:30 pm	Lunch
1:30 pm	Session 4: Friendships with Girls and Women
4:30 pm	Closure

DAY THREE

9.00 am	Session 5: The Quest for Identity
12:30 pm	Lunch
1:30 pm	Session 6: The Blessing Ritual
4:30 pm	Closure

Six-Day Fathers and Sons Hike

The *Between Fathers and Sons program* can be done on a six-day hike. Plan on walking between 15 and 20 kilometres per day, which should take about four or five hours depending on the terrain. The walking should be at a leisurely pace to allow for reflection and sharing.

The sessions are the same as the six-week program except that one topic is covered each day. This gives more time for reflection and sharing. It is good to walk in silence for at least the first hour of the day (and preferably the first two hours) to allow fathers and sons the chance to reflect deeply on the subject matter. Other preparations include:

Handouts, Equipment, Safety, Guide

Handouts: Photocopy the materials suggested for Days One to Five and the Blessing Ritual. Because fewer resources can be carried on a hike than would be used in other settings, the facilitators will need to adapt sessions.

Equipment: Hiking packs, walking boots, walking poles (optional), wet weather gear, water bottles, warm clothing, sunscreen, hats, food, tents, GPS, cooking facilities, socks, sleeping bags, ground sheets, underwear, toiletries, camera, blister kit, first aid kit, toilet paper, mobile phones, foot plan, maps, etc.

Safety and Guide: The route for the six-day hike needs to be carefully planned and the safety of fathers and sons emphasized (e.g., no going off on one's own). It would be ideal to have an experienced guide lead the group.

Briefing Meetings for Fathers and Sons

Conduct two Briefing Meetings at least one month prior to the six-day hike. Arrange for fathers and sons to give presentations as called for in the various sessions. Provide these volunteers with the appropriate resources from the Photocopy section and tell them on which day they will be making their presentations. Also, remind all the fathers to bring a photo of their sons as infants and to prepare a short remembrance of his birth or his first years for Session Five (Day Five). At the first Briefing Meeting ask the fathers and sons to bring their hiking gear to the second Briefing Meeting so that facilitators can make sure everyone is well equipped. Emphasize that the six days of hiking are not a race or a competition to see who is fittest.

Sample Schedule

DAY 1: THE FATHER AND SON BOND

6:00 am   Rise
- Begin packing up
- Make sure you have enough water for the day
- If you have blisters, put on plasters before you put on your socks and boots

7:00 am   Breakfast
- Finish packing up
- Make sure you don't leave anything behind at the campsite
- Put on a hat and sun screen – face, arms and legs
- Briefing on the specifics of the day's walk (the distance, the weather forecasr, where the group will stop for a snack, for toilet breaks, where the group will have lunch)

8:00 am   Day 1: The Father and Son Bond
- Introduction by the facilitators
- The stories of two fathers (Resource 4)

8:30 am   Begin walking in silence
- Personal Reflection: The Father and Son Bond (Resource 5)

9:30 am   Father and Sons Dialogue as they walk together
- Sharing about the Personal Reflection (Resource 5)

10:00 am   General conversation as the group walks

12:00 pm   Lunch

1:00 pm   Begin walking
- General conversation as the group walks

3:30 pm   Arrival at campsite
- Set up tents
- Prepare for dinner

6:00 pm   Dinner

7:30 pm   Group Sharing
- Guidelines for small group sharing (Resource 6)
- Day 1: Small Group Sharing Questions (Resource 7)
- Concluding prayer

9:30 pm   Sleep

DAY 2: BECOMING A MAN

6:00 am   Rise
- Begin packing up

7:00 am   Breakfast
- Finish packing up
- Briefing on the day's walk

8:00 am	Day 2: Becoming a Man	

- Introduction by the facilitators
- Understanding Archetypes (Resource 8)

8:30 am — Begin walking in silence
- Personal Reflection: Personality Profile (Resource 9)
- The Four Male Archetypes (Resource 10)

9:30 am — Father and Sons Dialogue as they walk together
- Sharing about the Personal Reflection (Resources 9 and 10))

10:00 am — General conversation as the group walks

12:00 pm — Lunch

1:00 pm — Begin walking
- General conversation as the group walks

3:30 pm — Arrival at campsite
- Set up tents
- Prepare for dinner

6:00 pm — Dinner

7:30 pm — Imagination Exercise: Searching for God
- Guidelines for small group sharing (Resource 6)
- Day 2: Small Group Sharing Questions (Resource 11)
- Concluding prayer

9:30 pm — Sleep

DAY 3: DEALING WITH ANGER

6:00 am — Rise
- Begin packing up

7:00 am — Breakfast
- Finish packing up
- Briefing on the day's walk

8:00 am — Day 3: Dealing with anger
- Introduction by the facilitators
- The stories of two fathers and two sons (Resource 12)
- Gospel: Jesus gets angry (John 2:13-17)

8:30 am — Begin walking in silence
- Personal Reflection: Dealing with Anger (Resource 14)

9:30 am — Father and Sons Dialogue as they walk together
- Sharing about the Personal Reflection (Resource 14)

10:00 am — General conversation as the group walks

12:00 pm — Lunch

1:00 pm	Begin walking	

- General conversation as the group walks

3:30 p m	Arrival at campsite	

- Set up tents
- Prepare for dinner

6:00 pm	Dinner
7:30 pm	Group Sharing

- Guidelines for small group sharing (Resource 6)
- Day 3: Small Group Sharing Questions (Resource 15)
- Concluding prayer

9:30 pm	Sleep

DAY 4:	**FRIENDSHIPS WITH GIRLS AND WOMEN**
6:00 am	Rise

- Begin packing up

7:00 am	Breakfast

- Finish packing up
- Briefing on the day's walk

8:00 am	Day 4: Friendships with girls and women

- Introduction by the facilitators
- Gospel: "I call you friends" (John 15:12-15)
- The stories of three fathers (Resource 16)

8:30 am	Begin walking in silence

- Reflection: Friendships with girls and women (Resource 17)

9:30 am	Father and Sons Dialogue as they walk together

- Sharing about the Personal Reflection (Resource 17)

10:00 am	General conversation as the group walks
12:00 pm	Lunch
1:00 pm	Begin walking

- General conversation as the group walks

3:30 p m	Arrival at campsite

- Set up tents
- Prepare for dinner

6:00 pm	Dinner
7:30 pm	Group Sharing

- Guidelines for small group sharing (Resource 6)
- Day 4: Small Group Sharing Questions (Resource 18)
- Concluding prayer

9:30 pm	Sleep

Appendix

DAY 5:	**THE QUEST FOR IDENTITY**	

6:00 am   Rise
- Begin packing up

7:00 am   Breakfast
- Finish packing up
- Briefing on the day's walk

8:00 am   Day 5: The quest for identity
- Introduction by the facilitators
- The stories of three sons (Resource 19)

8:30 am   Begin walking in silence
- Reflection: My Life History (Resource 21)

9:30 am   Father and Sons Dialogue as they walk together
- Sharing about My Life History (Resource 21)

10:00 am   General conversation as the group walks

12:00 pm   Lunch

1:00 pm   Begin walking
- General conversation as the group walks

3:30 pm   Arrival at campsite
- Set up tents
- Prepare for dinner

6:00 pm   Dinner

7:30 pm   Group Sharing
- Guidelines for small group sharing (Resource 6)
- Day 5: Small Group Sharing Questions (Resource 20)
- Concluding prayer

9:30 pm   Sleep

DAY 6:	**THE BLESSING RITUAL**	

6:00 am   Rise
- Begin packing up

7:00 am   Breakfast
- Finish packing up
- Briefing on the day's walk

8:00 am   Day 6: The Blessing Ritual
- Introduction by the facilitators
- Examination of Father and Son Relationships

8:30 am   Begin walking in silence
- Reflection: The hurtful times in the father-son relationship

9:30 am	Father and Sons Dialogue as they walk together
	• Sharing about the Personal Reflection
10:00 am	General conversation as the group walks
12:00 pm	Lunch
1:00 pm	Begin walking
	• General conversation as the group walks
3:30 pm	Arrival at campsite
	• Set up tents
	• Prepare for dinner
6:00 pm	Dinner
7:30 pm	Blessing Ritual
	• Foot washing ceremony (if possible)
	• Reading letters of affirmation
9:30 pm	Sleep

Notes

Introduction

1. Richard Rohr and Joseph Martos, *The Wild Man's Journey: Reflections on Male Spirituality*, Cincinnati, Ohio: St. Anthony Messenger Press, 1992, 50.

2. Satyanshu Mukherjee, *Juvenile Crime: Overview of Changing Patterns* (Australian Institute of Criminology). http://www.aic.gov.au/events/aic%20upcoming%20events/1997/~/media/conferences/juvenile/mukherjee.pdf

3. Ibid.

4. Australian Institute of Criminology, *Data on Policing and Arrests*. http://www.aic.gov.au/en/publications/current%20series/rpp/100-120/rpp107/04.aspx

5. Robert Moore and Douglas Gillette, *King, Warrior, Magician and Lover: Rediscovering the Arche- types of the Mature Masculine*, San Francisco: HarperCollins Publishers, 1990, xvi.

6. Mircea Eliade, *Rites and Symbols of Initiation: The Mysteries of Birth and Rebirth*, New York: Harper and Row, Publishers, 1975, 3.

Briefing Meeting for Fathers and Sons

7. This story is quoted by Brian Cavanaugh in *More Sower's Seeds: Second Planting*, New York: Paulist Press, 1992, 16.

Session Three: Dealing with Anger

8. The research mentioned appears in John Gottman's book, *Why Marriages Succeed or Fail*, New York: Simon and Schuster, 1994.

9. Adapted from the prayer exercise "Release from Resentment," by Anthony de Mello, SJ, in *Sadhana: A Way to God*, Anand, India: Gujarat Sahitya Prakash, 1988, 83ff.

Session Five: The Quest for Identity

10. Carlos Valles, *Tales of the City of God*, Anand, India: Gujarat Sahitya Prakash, 1992, 80ff.

Further Resources

Alberti, Robert E. and Michael L. Emmons *Your Perfect Right: A Guide to Assertive Living*. San Luis Obispo, California: Impact Publishers, 1987.

Bettelheim, Bruno. *The Uses of Enchantment: The Meaning and Importance of Fairy Tales*. New York: Vintage Books, 1989.

Bly, Robert. *Iron John: A Book About Men*. New York: Addison-Wesley Publishing Co., 1990.

Campbell, Alastair V. *The Gospel of Anger*. London: SPCK, 1986.

de Mello, Anthony. *Sadhana: A Way to God*. Anand, India: Gujarat Sahitya Prakash, 1988.

Erikson, Erik H. *Identity and the Life Cycle*. New York: W.W. Norton and Company, 1980.

Guzie, Tad, and Noreen Monroe Guzie. *About Men and Women: How Your "Great Story" Shapes Your Destiny.* New York: Paulist Press, 1986.

Mahdi, Louise Carus, Stephen Foster, and Meredith Little, eds. *Betwixt and Between: Patterns of Masculine and Feminine Initiation.* La Salle, Illinois: Open Court, 1987.

Mitscherlich, Alexander. *Society without the Father.* New York: Harper Perennial, 1993.

Moore, Robert and Douglas Gillette. *King, Warrior, Magician, Lover: Rediscovering the Archetypes of the Mature Masculine.* San Francisco: HarperCollins Publishers, 1990.

Moore, Robert and Douglas Gillette. *The King Within: Accessing the King Within the Male Psyche.* New York: William Morrow and Company, Inc., 1992.

Moore, Robert and Douglas Gillette. *The Warrior Within: Accessing the Knight in the Male Psyche.* New York: William Morrow and Company, Inc., 1992.

Osherson, Samuel. *Finding Our Fathers: How a Man's Life Is Shaped by His Relationship with His Father.* New York: Fawcett Columbine, 1986.

Raphael, Ray. *The Men from the Boys: Rites of Passage in Male America.* Lincoln: University of Nebraska Press, 1988.

Rohr, Richard, and Joseph Martos. *The Wildman's Journey: Reflections on Male Spirituality.* Cincinnati, Ohio: St. Anthony Messenger Press, 1992.

Scull, Charles, ed. *Fathers, Sons and Daughters.* Los Angeles: Jeremy P. Tarcher, Inc., 1992.

Valles, Carlos. *Tales of the City of God,* Anand, India: Gujarat Sahitya Prakash, 1992

Photocopy Resource Section

Multiple copies of the following pages are needed for the *Between Fathers and Sons* program (see the individual sessions for specific instructions on the use of the materials). These pages may be photocopied for your convenience for distribution during the sessions.

Between Fathers and Sons

A program for adolescent males and their fathers

Briefing Meeting for Fathers and Sons

Date:

Time:

Location:

The Process

The process for the six sessions includes a sharing of common experiences, times for private dialogue between fathers and sons, sharing in small groups, gospel reflections, and fun.

Regular pot luck meals at each session add to the spirit of welcome and open communication.

Boys without Fathers

Many adolescent males do not live with or near their fathers. If this is the case, it is still possible for the teen to participate in the program. Mentors, such as an adult male relative, stepfather, or member of the faith community, may take the place of the father in this program. Please let us know if you or your son needs help in finding a mentor.

Some of the goals for the *Between Fathers and Sons* program

- To open or maintain the lines of communication between fathers and sons
- To help fathers and sons build on their relationship with trust
- To examine some positive ways fathers can help their sons enter into manhood
- To image God as a loving Father
- To develop healthy ways of reponding to anger
- To help teens learn skills for building friendships with girls and women
- To help fathers and sons to name and claim their deepest life aspirations
- To allow fathers and sons the opportunity to mutually affirm one another

If you are interested in finding out more about the *Between Fathers and Sons* program, please plan to attend the Briefing Meeting for Fathers and Sons. For more information call:

Phone:

Session 1:
The Father and Son Bond

Fathers have a crucial role in helping their adolescent sons make the transition from boyhood into manhood. This session helps to develop a secure environment where fathers and sons can relate openly and honestly with one another. A purpose of this session is to recognize the importance of love, trust, respect, and communication between fathers and sons and to add to and build upon them.

Date and time:

Session 2:
Becoming a Man

While this session identifies many of the changes an adolescent boy faces in becoming a man, its focus is on one aspect of his personality that remains fairly constant—in psychological terms, his archetype. The male archetypes—father, seeker, warrior, sage—are part of each man's personality, present from birth, that influence his behavior and the dynamics of his relationships. When fathers and sons identify primarily with different archetypes, difficulties and tensions often arise that can be eased when each learns to recognize and affirm the other's dreams and motivations as well as his own.

Date and time:

Session 3:
Dealing with Anger

Boys need their fathers to model for them the crucial task of positively channeling anger. This session provides time for the fathers and sons to share what causes them to feel angry, how they deal with their anger, and how they can cope constructively with any tendencies they might have toward negative responses to anger, including violence and passivity.

Date and time:

Session 4:
Friendships with Girls and Women

Boys are usually adept in making friends with other males, but need encouragement to transfer these skills to forming friendships with females. Shyness and a propensity among peers to treat females with disrespect adds to the difficulty teenage boys may have making friends with girls. This session provides some helpful hints and allows fathers to share with their sons some of their own attitudes toward the women in their lives.

Date and time:

Session 5:
The Quest for Identity

Achieving self-identity means coming up with a clear answer to the question "Who am I?" In this session fathers help their sons fill in the missing pieces of their life stories by sharing with them remembrances of their birth and early years. The sons respond by sharing with their fathers some of their dreams and aspirations for the future.

Date and time:

Session 6:
The Blessing Ritual

Adolescent males need to be noticed, affirmed, admired, and delighted in by their fathers. They need to relate on an intimate level with their fathers and receive from them a sense of personal validation as men. A term for this affirmation is *blessing*. Set in the context of familiar liturgical rites, this prayer celebration is a true affirmation of fathers and sons, and their growing relationship.

Date and time:

Fathers and Sons Program Timetable

Session 1: The Father and Son Bond

Date _____   Time _____

Session 2: Becoming a Man

Date _____   Time _____

Session 3: Dealing with Anger

Date _____   Time _____

Session 4: Friendships with Girls and Women

Date _____   Time _____

Session 5: The Quest for Identity

Date _____   Time _____

Session 6: The Blessing Ritual

Date _____   Time _____

Father Information Sheet

Name: _____

Age: _____

Occupation: _____

Home Address: _____

Home Phone Number: _____

Mobile Number: _____

How you heard about the program: _____

Your son or mentee's name: _____

✂--

Son Information Sheet

Name: _____

Age: _____

School: _____

Home Address: _____

Home Phone Number: _____

Mobile Number: _____

How you heard about the program: _____

Your father or mentor's name: _____

Resource 2

Casual Meal Sign Up

Session 1 Date:

Salad   _____ / _____ / _____

Main Course   _____ / _____ / _____

Dessert   _____ / _____ / _____

Session 2 Date:

Salad   _____ / _____ / _____

Main Course   _____ / _____ / _____

Dessert   _____ / _____ / _____

Session 3 Date:

Salad   _____ / _____ / _____

Main Course   _____ / _____ / _____

Dessert   _____ / _____ / _____

Session 4 Date:

Salad   _____ / _____ / _____

Main Course   _____ / _____ / _____

Dessert   _____ / _____ / _____

Session 5 Date:

Salad   _____ / _____ / _____

Main Course   _____ / _____ / _____

Dessert   _____ / _____ / _____

The Father and Son Bond

Session One introduces the importance of the father and son relationship in assisting the proper development of sons from adolescence to manhood. We will emphasise particularly the importance of trust in the father-son relationship. Your five-minute talk about your own father will be an important part of the session. A well-prepared talk will help the other fathers and sons in their reflections.

For your talk, it will be helpful to share some personal stories about your father and how you got along with him. Make your talk personal. This can be done by using quite a few "I" statements. Use the following sentence starters to help you. You do not have to include all the statements in your talk.

Sentence Starters

- When I was a boy, my father . . .
- Sometimes I see glimpses of my father in me when . . .
- When I think of my father I feel . . .
- I would describe my relationship with my father as . . .
- I learned I could trust my father when . . .
- My image of God was shaped by my image of my father in that . . .

You might also answer the following questions:

Questions

- What is my first memory of my father?
- What were/are my father's outstanding qualities?
- What were/are my father's most difficult characteristics?
- How am I unlike my father? How am I like him?
- How did my father share his faith with me?

You might like to bring an object with you that symbolises your father and tell why this is so.

Personal Reflection: The Father and Son Bond

Directions: Read through each of the following exercises. Then choose and complete *one* of the exercises in the space below.

- **Write** a continuation to the parable of the father and the two sons. What do you think happened at the party?

- What did you find most interesting in the talks given by the two fathers? **Write** about one insight you gained from their presentations.

- **Draw** yourself and your father. Or, **draw** the objects you and your father were holding in the imagination exercise.

- Conduct a flow of consciousness. This means you simply **write** down as many words as you can think of that describe your father and your relationship with him.

Guidelines for Small Group Sharing

- Read through the list of sharing questions and sentence starters. Take the first five minutes of your time together to think of stories or personal examples you can use to illustrate your responses. Rank them in order from 1 to 5, with 1 being the question you feel most willing to share with the group. This should be done as quietly as possible.

- Go around the group sharing your responses to the question you ranked number 1. One person speaks at a time. Feel free to say as much or as little as you please, keeping in mind the time limit and the need for everyone to have the opportunity to share.

- Do not interrupt while another person speaks. Be an attentive listener, giving your full attention to the speaker. Be very careful not to analyse, or give advice, or make comments on what has been shared. If you are unclear about what a person means, you may ask a clarifying question, but this should not develop into a general discussion. Small group sharing is not a discussion or dialogue time.

- All sharing must be done freely. If at any time a person does not wish to share a response with the group, the person simply says "pass". If a person does choose to respond, however, the response should always be as honest as possible.

- If there is time after everyone has shared one response, go around the group again sharing a second response.

- Leave five minutes at the end of the session to offer positive comments about what you heard. Go around the group sharing a brief comment to one of the following:

    — a piece of meaningful advice that was shared;

    — something positive you will do as a result of something you heard;

    — a word of encouragement to one of the speakers.

Session 1 Small Group Sharing Questions

Directions: Read through the list of questions. Decide how you can respond to each one. Write your responses or take notes to help you remember. Then rank the questions from 1 to 5 with 1 being the question you are most willing to share with the group.

- What is the first memory I have of my father? (What is the first memory I have of my son?)

- When was a time my father-son relationship needed forgiveness and reconciliation, like the gospel story of the father with two sons?

- When was a time I trusted my father? (When was a time I trusted my son?) What did I learn about trust from this incident?

- How am I like my father? How am I different from my father? (How am I like my son? How am I different from my son?)

- How do I envision my relationship with my father in 10 years? (How do I envision my relationship with my son in 10 years?)

Understanding Archetypes

ICEBERG

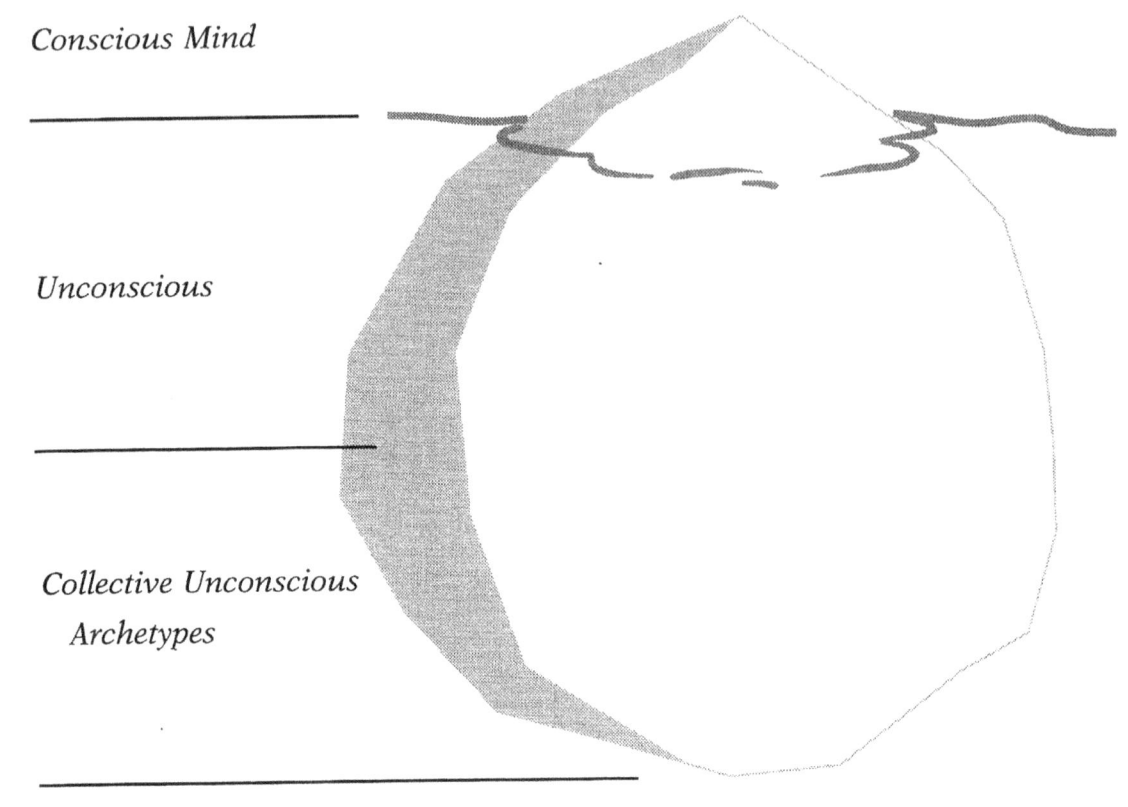

Conscious Mind

Unconscious

*Collective Unconscious
Archetypes*

Four **male archetypes** are:

        Father

        Seeker

        Warrior

        Sage

Personality Profile

Directions: Listed below are some common characteristics of the four male archetypes. Indicate how much each characteristic describes you by the following scale:

    V—very much

    S—somewhat

    N—not much

1. I enjoy being with and doing things with my family or with a particular group of friends. _____
2. I like to do things my own way. _____
3. Efficiency is my trademark. _____
4. I am a deep thinker. _____
5. I am usually satisfied with things as they've always been. _____
6. I am naturally open-minded. _____
7. I am extremely goal-oriented. _____
8. I have been called "absent minded". _____
9. I like to pass on what I know to others. _____
10. I seek a variety of friendships. _____
11. I like to be in control of all areas of my life, including relationships. _____
12. I prefer the sharing of ideas to competition. _____
13. I like to be asked for help. _____
14. I feel stifled by the traditions and customs of family, society, religion. _____
15. Winning is important to me. _____
16. I have been described as "wise" or "wise for my age".

	V	S	N	Total
Father				
Seeker				
Warrior				
Sage				

The Four Male Archetypes

A person with a **father** archetype finds his identity in providing for and protecting others. The father likes to care for others. You don't have to ever have children of your own to have this archetype. The father is not concerned with power for its own sake. Rather he uses his power to protect his brood—family, friendship group, employees—from anything threatening. The father enjoys being with his "family". The father is the guardian of tradition and convention. He values stability, permanence, and the status quo. He wants to pass on to others what has worked well for him. Naturally conservative, he thinks, "What has helped me in the past will help you now".

While the father is satisfied with "things as they have always been," the **seeker** wants to explore, to try new ways. He is often very creative. His life is one of searching and questing. He likes to do his own thing. While the father is concerned with the traditions of the group—family, organisations, religion, etc.—the seeker feels stifled by them. The seeker acts as if rules don't apply to him. Instead, he develops his own set of rules that mostly protect his freedom to be a seeker. Negatively, the seeker can be irresponsible and never grow up. At his best, he may "boldly go where no one has gone before".

A person with primarily a **warrior** archetype is one who sets goals and achieves them. The warrior enjoys competition and is not afraid of a struggle or a fight. Efficiency is his trademark. The warrior's goals always come first. The warrior archetype is socially acceptable for a man in his 20s and 30s because he is meant to be a man with the drive to get things done. Because a warrior is energised by what is achievable, he often has little patience for people who live by values other than efficiency. He sometimes has trouble with relationships. For the warrior, the task comes first, relationships second.

The **sage** is known as a thinker. He is constantly developing a coherent, personal philosophy of life that he feels others need too. Therefore he is always attempting to articulate what he believes so that others will understand. For the sage "meaning" takes precedence over "doing", so even in a busy meeting where important decisions have to be made, or during a class where a paper has to be written, you may find the sage daydreaming to himself or philosophising to others. A sage often plays a vital role in the advancement of ideas and the improvement of society, but he may need more practical people to make his ideas work. Hence the description "absent minded professor" is often associated with the sage.

Session 2 Small Group Sharing Questions

Directions: Read through the list of questions. Decide how you can respond to each one. Write your responses or take notes to help you remember. Then rank the questions from 1 to 5 with 1 being the question you are most willing to share with the group.

- In the imagination exercise, where was the place you were led to in the city in your search for God? What significance or symbolism do you think this place has for you?

- What was the symbol you chose for God? How did you feel when you stood before the symbol? How did you feel when you became the symbol and looked at yourself standing there?

- How did you think of God when you were a child? How has your image of God changed? What does having a personal relationship with God have to do with becoming a man?

- Jesus told us of a God who is a loving Father. How does this image of God work for you? What are some characteristics of your father or another father you know that have helped you to understand and experience God?

- Tell some ways that your understanding of male archetypes can help you or help your son in the process of becoming a man.

Dealing with Anger

Session Three explores the feeling of anger and how men express this feeling. In the session, it will be pointed out that of itself, anger is neither good nor bad. Rather, it is how one handles his anger that can have good or bad implications.

The presentations of two father and son pairs will be a cornerstone of the session. A well-prepared presentation will help all the fathers and sons in their own reflections.

The total presentation time for each father and son pair is 10 minutes. You might choose to work together as a team and refer to each other in some way during your presentation. Or, you may prefer to give your talks separately (e.g., two five-minute talks).

The focus of your presentation is how you deal with anger. Please make your presentation personal. This can be done by using "I" statements. Use the following sentence starters to help you. You do not have to include all the statements in your talk.

Sentence Starters

- When I feel angry I . . .
- One time I physically struck another person when I was angry and I . . .
- I find my anger difficult to control when . . .
- The way my father (son) handles anger is . . .
- A positive way I handle my anger is . . .
- Something that makes me very angry is . . .

You might also answer the following questions:

Questions

- What makes me angry?
- Where in my body do I feel angry?
- When was the time I was most angry?
- When was my father angriest with me? How did he handle the anger?

You might also wish to touch on the larger subject of violence in our society, especially in the area of violence toward women.

Dealing with Anger Role Plays

Scene 1

A teacher accuses **Mark** of talking in class and gives him detention. Actually, the teacher has targeted the wrong student.

Teacher: Mark, stop talking and pay attention! You know the consequences; here's a detention for you. (Hands Mark a piece of paper.)

Mark: (sarcastically, and under his breath) Yeah, right.

Mark crumples up the detention and puts it in his pocket. The teacher continues the lesson.

Teacher: Could anyone explain for me the Pythagorean Theorem? Mark, you did well on your last exam. How about you?

Mark: (emotionless) No.

Scene 2

A teacher accuses **Ben** of talking in class and gives him detention. Actually, the teacher has targeted the wrong student.

Teacher: Ben, stop talking and pay attention! You know the consequences. I'll see you after school at detention. (Hands Ben a piece of paper.)

Ben refuses to take the paper.

Ben: (screaming) Hey, I wasn't the one talking! Who do you think you are? You can wait all night if you want, but you'll never see me here after school.

Ben storms out of the room, slamming the door behind him.

Scene 3

A teacher accuses **Frank** of talking in class and gives him a detention. Actually, the teacher has targeted the wrong student.

Teacher: Frank, stop talking and pay attention! You know the consequences. I'll see you at detention. (Hands Frank a piece of paper.)

Frank says nothing in response. A bell rings (make a ringing sound) signifying the end of the class period. Frank approaches the teacher respectfully.

Frank: Excuse me, Mr. Smith, may I speak to you for a moment? You gave me detention for talking, but I wasn't the one talking. I don't think this detention is fair. (Hands paper back to teacher.)

Teacher: Well I suppose I could have made a mistake. Actually, I could only tell the talking was coming from your area, and I was really frustrated by it. I'm sorry. Don't worry about this. (Puts paper in desk or pocket.)

Frank: Thanks, Mr. Smith. See you tomorrow.

Personal Reflection: Dealing with Anger

Directions: Read through each of the following exercises. Then choose and complete *one* of the exercises in the space below.

- **Write** your impressions of Jesus' response to the sellers and money-changers. Why do you think he acted as he did?

- What did you find most interesting in the talks given by the fathers and sons? How were their experiences like your own? Different from your own? **Write** about one insight you gained from their presentations.

- **Draw** a symbol of your anger. Or, **draw** the way you usually respond when angry.

- Conduct a flow of consciousness. This means you simply **write** down as many words as you can think of that describe your angry feelings and the ways you deal with anger.

Session 3 Small Group Sharing Scenarios

Directions: Read each scenario. Offer suggestions for passive, aggressive, and assertive ways to respond. Then tell how *you* would likely respond if . . .

   . . . you are a **father** and your son returns your car to you with a nearly empty petrol tank.

   . . . you are a **son** and your father approaches your coach after a game and demands that he increase your playing time.

   . . . you are a **father** and your son's mathematics grade drops from a B to a D over the course of eight weeks.

   . . . you are a **son** and your father gives you a weekend curfew that is an hour earlier than most of your friends.

   . . . you are a **father** and your son talks back to his mother.

   . . . you are a **son** and your father picks up the other phone while you are talking with a friend, waits about 10 seconds, and then tells you it's time to hang up.

   . . . you are a **father** and your son is a part of a group of teenagers which has thrown toilet paper and eggs at a classmate's house.

   . . . you are a **son** and your father drinks too many beers at a neighbour's barbeque and then insists on driving home.

   . . . you are a **father** and you find marijuana rolling papers in your son's room.

   . . . you are a **son** and your father calls you lazy because you don't have an after-school job.

   . . . you are a **father** and your son takes his girlfriend to his bedroom and closes his door.

   . . . you are a **son** and your father constantly criticises your mother.

Friendships with Girls and Women

Session Four is about friendship between men and women. Your personal presentation will be a key part of the session. A well-prepared presentation will help the other fathers and sons in their reflections.

In your five-minute presentation, please share some personal stories about how you have related to women as friends and with respect. This session does not particularly address the area of sexuality and its implications in man and woman relationships, though you may touch on those issues if you wish. You can tell about relationships with many women who are and have been a part of your life: mother, grandmothers, sisters, girlfriends, wife, daughters, co-workers, and so on.

Also, many teenage boys have trouble getting to know girls. Though attracted to girls, shyness is a major stumbling block. You might include some reminiscence of the difficulties you first had in making friends with girls and some techniques you had for overcoming shyness.

Remember to make your presentation personal. This can be achieved by using quite a few "I" statements in your talk. Use the following sentence starters to help you. You do not have to include all the statements in your talk.

Sentence Starters

- My grandmother was . . .
- My mother and I . . .
- I learned to overcome my shyness with girls by . . .
- I remember my first girlfriend because . . .
- When I first met my wife I thought . . .
- When my wife and I were dating some of the best times were . . .
- My wife is my best friend because . . .
- My daughter is special to me because . . .
- I enjoy having women as friends because . . .
- I believe that women should be treated with respect because . . .
- My relationship with women friends is different than with men friends because . . .
- A lesson I learned from my mother is . . .
- A lesson I learned from my wife is . . .
- A lesson I learned from my daughter is . . .

Also, you may wish to include in your presentation personal reflections on the following issues:

- The emotional and physical differences between a man and a woman, and the importance of respecting those differences.
- The importance of respecting a woman's prerogative to say "no", especially in the area of sexual relations.

Resource 16

Personal Reflection: Friendships with Girls and Women

Directions: Read through each of the following exercises. Then choose and complete *one* of the exercises in the space below.

- **Write** about the best friend you thought of in the imagination exercise. Tell why you consider this person to be your best friend.

- Who is a person you recently developed a friendship with? What are some techniques you use to make new friends? How can these techniques and the ones you heard in the presentation help you to form friendships with females. **Write** about one insight you gained from the presentations and answer the questions above.

- **Write** the initials of five females you are currently friends with or would like to be friends with. Next to each set of initials, write one practical strategy you can use for maintaining the friendships or becoming friends.

- Conduct a flow of consciousness. This means you simply **write** down as many words you can think of that describe how you can show respect for a woman in your relationship with her.

Session 4 Small Group Sharing Questions

Directions: Read through the list of questions. Decide how you can respond to each one. Write your responses or take notes to help you remember. Then rank the questions from 1 to 5 with 1 being the question you are most willing to share with the group.

- Tell about a person or an incident that helped you learn something about the true meaning of friendship.

- Generally, how do you think males your age feel about females?

- What types of pressures do teenage boys face when they attempt to start friendships with females? What can be done to alleviate those pressures?

- What qualities of friendship are most important to you?

- List several characteristics of girls or women that you find attractive.

The Quest for Identity

The theme for Session Five involves the "quest for personal identity". This entails looking into the future and imagining the kind of person you would like to become and the impact you hope to have on the world. Your personal presentation on this theme will be an important part of the process. A well-prepared presentation will help other sons and fathers in their reflections.

Please plan to speak for five minutes. Make your presentation personal. This can be achieved by using quite a few "I" statements in your talk. Use the following sentence starters to help you. You do not have to include all the statements in your talk.

Sentence Starters

- When I was younger I dreamed of becoming a . . .
- I believe I have a talent for . . .
- People have told me that I would be good at . . .
- My ultimate dream is to . . .
- I envision myself as the kind of Christian who . . .
- I think I would make a good husband and father because . . .

Or, you may wish to address the following questions during your presentation:

- What sort of man will I be 10 years from now? 20 years from now? 30 years from now?
- What do I hope will be my greatest lifetime achievement?
- Who does God want me to be?
- What is my Christian vocation?

Session 5 Small Group Sharing of Memories

For Fathers

Directions: You are to share a particular memory about the time before your son's birth, the day of his birth, or his infancy. If you wish, base your memory on one of the following notes. Begin your talk by passing around the photo of your son.

- Talk about the day you found out you were going to be a father.
- What preparations did you make for your son's birth?
- Describe what you did the hours before your son's birth, the time of his birth, and the hours after his birth.
- What behavioural or personality trait has been present in your son since he was a baby?
- How did you choose your son's name?
- Talk about your son's first night home from the hospital.
- What were your son's first words? When did he walk?
- Talk about a time you felt proud to be the father of your son.

For Sons

Directions: You are to share one of your earliest memories of times spent with your father. If you wish, base your memory on one of the following notes.

- What is your earliest memory of your father?
- Describe the first home you remember living in.
- Talk about the first time you remember your father taking you to his work.
- What is something you remember your father teaching you as a child?
- What is a story you heard your mother or other relatives tell about your father when you were younger?
- What was a special time you and your father used to share together when you were a young child?
- What is something your father did to make you angry when you were younger?
- What is something your father did that made you feel proud of him when you were younger?

Personal Reflection: My Life History

Directions: Write words or draw symbols representing the high and low points of your life to your current age and picturing your dreams and aspirations for the future.

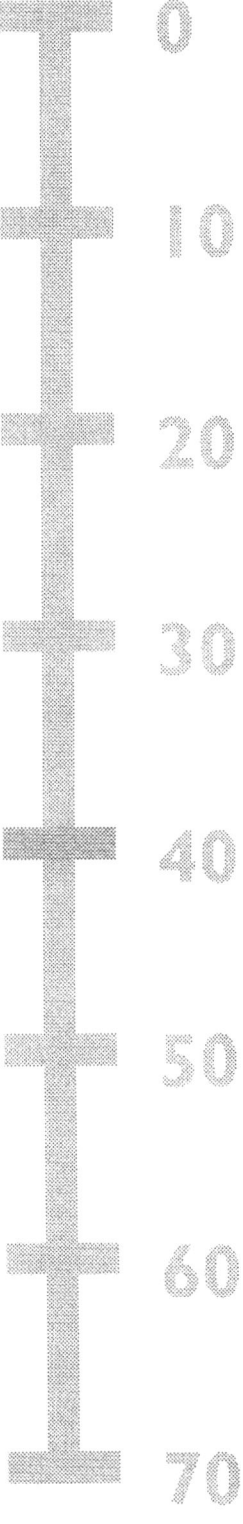

Resource 21

Program Evaluation

Please evaluate the *Between Fathers and Sons* program and your participation in it (use the back of the paper, if necessary). You will have about 10 minutes.

List some things you liked about the *Between Fathers and Sons* program, and tell what you liked about them. *Suggestions:* meal-sharing, gospel reflections, imagination exercises, father and son dialogue, personal reflection, small group sharing, etc.

What are some suggestions you can offer for improving the *Between Fathers and Sons* program?

What is one way your relationship with your father or son has changed during your time in this program?

Prayer of Affirmation

For Fathers

Directions: Write a prayer for your son. Your prayer can be addressed to God written for your son or simply a letter to your son. Use several "I" statements to make your prayer more personal. For example:

- When you were a young boy, I loved to . . .
- Your birth was meaningful to me because . . .
- I admire the way you . . .
- I am proud that you are my son because . . .
- I love you . . .

You may also wish to mention some of the qualities your son possesses. For example:

| gentleness | kindness | respect | truthfulness | humility | responsibility |
| patience | openness | forgiveness | love | justice | courage |

Prayer of Affirmation

For Sons

Directions: Write a prayer for your father. Your prayer can be addressed to God written for your father or simply a letter to your father. Use several "I" statements to make your prayer more personal. For example:

- I really appreciate . . .
- I admire the way you . . .
- I am glad you are my father because . . .
- I hope I can be a man like you because . . .
- I love you . . .

You may also wish to mention some of the qualities your father possesses. For example:

| gentleness | kindness | respect | truthfulness | humility | responsibility |
| patience | openness | forgiveness | love | justice | courage |

Resource 23

NOTES

NOTES

NOTES

NOTES

www.ingramcontent.com/pod-product-compliance
Lightning Source LLC
Chambersburg PA
CBHW082015220426

43671CB00014B/2583